Helping You Train Your

Children To Live For The

Glory of God!

Published by Mission Minded Publishers for UnveilinGLORY
© 2015 ❖ Sjogren and Sjogren
First Printing, 2015

ISBN: 978-0-9862066-1-0

To order additional copies, contact UnveilinGLORY at 804.781.0386

Printed in the *United States of America*

Photograph of the kitten was by: Marie-Lan Nguyen via Wikimedia Commons.

Photograph of the puppy was by: Helena Hybnerova, Legendary Hills, via Wikimedia Commons.

How to Use this Manual...

The Parent's Guidebook is to be used with *The Children's Workbook*. This guide helps you direct your child as to what activities they are to do each day in *The Children's Workbook*.

The entire curriculum is divided into 30 weeks. Each week has 3 lessons. This means that there are 90 lessons for your children to work through. (You can keep track by watching the Weeks/Days or Lessons.) It is designed to last approximately one, full, school year and work in tandem with the curriculum for teenagers.

Many times you will be discussing various topics with your child. All discussion questions are marked with a gray box:

> ***Discuss:*** Ask your child...

Along with this guidebook, you should have the following:
- *The Children's Workbook* (one per child.)
- *I Heard Good News Today 2: Big Life*
- *102 Differences Between Cats and Dogs for Kids!* (Cartoon Book)
- Cat and Dog Theology Audio CD for Kids
- *Because He Liked It* (A Cartoon Book by Gerald Robison)

(By the way, all of the stories in *I Heard Good News Today 2: Big Life* are **true stories** and most have happened since the year 2004. The people you are reading about are still alive and continue to minister today. Always feel free to pray for them.)

Each week has three lessons. Each day has the same format and should take ten to fifteen minutes.

Day 1:
- From *The Parent's Guidebook*, you will teach and discuss simple concepts for the kids to understand. **This teaching will be the theme for the week.**
- Once you have done this, you will then direct them to their workbook. There is a place for them to write out the verse each week. It is encouraged that they work on the verse throughout the week in order to memorize it.
- After the Scripture has been written out, you will then sing the Isaiah 28:6 theme song with the Audio CD (see page VIII).
- Then pray a prayer found on the "Prayer to Go" website. It has been written out for you so you don't have to search for it. But you can go to www.PrayerToGo.com and click on the Kids icon (seen at the right) and find the prayer and click on it to listen to it. There are 50 prayers on the web-

site. Only 30 are used in this curriculum.
- Finally, you will have them work on the activity found in their workbook. This ranges from crafts and games to songs.
- (There is an optional activity for those who want more to do!)

Day 2:
- Answer the reflection question in *The Children's Workbook*.
- Discuss the cartoon on the next page about what the Cat and Dog might be saying. Have your child fill in what he/she thinks the Cat and Dog might be saying and discuss the answer. (The answer is found in the cartoon book itself and the page will be given to you. You may want to look at this ahead of time to guide your child's answer if needed.) ***Please note, there is an additional question at the top of each cartoon; feel free to ask that question as well!***
- Find the story from *I Heard Good News Today 2: Big Life (IHGNT2: BL)*.
- In *The Children's Workbook*, note which country is being referenced.
- Then on page IX of *IHGNT2: BL*, have them point out the country they are reading about. (Also use page 181 of *The Children's Workbook* when it gets too easy on page IX of *IHGNT2: BL*.)
- Read the story.
- Discuss and have your child write the answer to the question regarding how the main character made God famous.
- Pray for the people of that country.
- (There is an optional activity for those who want more to do!)

Day 3:
- (The same as Day 2)

If you are interested in going deeper as the parent, please read ***Cat and Dog Theology*** by Bob Sjogren and Gerald Robison. This is the foundation for the first 15 weeks of material. ***God's Bottom Line,*** by Bob Sjogren, is the basis for the second 15 weeks of material. All can be purchased through www.UnveilinGLORY. com/Bookstore.

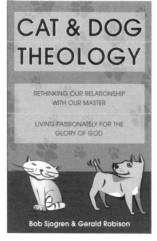
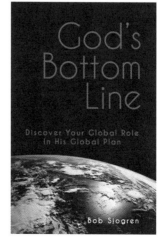

Table of Contents

Page #

Isaiah 26:8, Our Theme Song:

"We Want To Make God Famous!"

Hi Moms and Dads!
We've created an original song for this curriculum.
It is 2 minutes and 25 seconds long.
You'll find it on the Audio CD, Track 1.
There are three verses for you to sing.
(The words are on page 196 in
The Children's Workbook.)

In the first verse, you'll be singing with
Miss Elise's class in the Middle East.

In verses two and three,
you'll be singing with Holly Bard
and Brock and Faith Henderson.

If you think you've got it and want to try it on your own,
go to Track 13 and trying singing
with only the music!

Bob

Week 1- Making God Famous

I. Teaching:

We are about to learn a very important lesson about God, but it is all based on a joke that describes the differences between cats and dogs. A lesson about God that talks about cats and dogs? Sounds crazy, right?

> ***Discuss:*** Do you like dogs? What about cats?

And it is all based on a joke. Are you ready for the joke?

> A dog says, "You pet me, you feed me, you shelter me,
> you love me, ***you must be God.***"

> A cat says, "You pet me, you feed me, you shelter me,
> you love me, ***I must be God.***"

So while a dog lives to please and serve his master, a cat thinks the master is there to please and serve him.

> ***Discuss:*** If you have cats and dogs, do you see these traits in your pets? How? What about when you come home from a trip—how does a dog greet you? A cat? Or when you give a command—is a dog or cat more likely to obey?

Unfortunately, these different attitudes can describe many Christians today. There are some Christians, like dogs, who live to please and serve God. They want to make Him famous. But there are many Christians, like cats, who think God is there to make them happy and do everything they want. Now these "Cat Christians" would never say this, but they live as though they are god, with a small "g." They think life is all about them. They want God to make them look good.

Sometimes, Cats act as though God is like Santa Claus, someone who is here to give them whatever they want!

> ***Discuss:*** How else do Christians act like cats? What are some ways you've seen with your own life or your friends or in your church? How have you seen someone act like a "Dog Christian"?

The goal of this curriculum is to help you move from a Cat attitude, thinking God is there to please you, to a Dog attitude, living to please God and make Him famous.

II. Memory Verse:

Our memory verse for this week is Isaiah 26:8, "Yes, LORD, walking in the way of your laws, we wait for you; your name and renown *(fame)* are the desire of our hearts." (NIV)

> ***Discuss:*** Talk about what the verse means with your child.

III. Theme Song:

Play Track 1 on the Cat and Dog Audio CD provided in this kit. Have your kids sing along with our curriculum theme song, "We Want To Make God Famous!" See page 196 for the words.

IV. Prayer to Go:

Conclude today's teaching with praying Prayer to Go #11, all about glorifying and praising the Lord. (You can either listen to it on the internet or pray the words below.)

"Glorify the Lord with me and let us exalt His name together." Psalm 34:3

Dear Lord, Only You are worthy to be praised. You are perfect, all-powerful, all-wise, right in all you do, faithful, loving, kind, full of mercy, good, holy, majestic, gracious and so much more. Only You are worthy to be praised.

V. The Children's Workbook *(Page 1, 2)*:

To finish the day, have your child open to Week 1: Lesson 1 in the Cat & Dog Children's Workbook. Students will write out the weekly verse and complete the "Discover A Secret Message" activity page. **(Answers: David defeats Goliath / God Saves Daniel / An Ax Floats / God Parts The Red Sea / Solomon Had Great Wisdom / The Youngest Is Chosen / Boaz Redeems Ruth / Joseph Rises To Power)**

VI. Optional Activity:

Find the song "Famous One" by Chris Tomlin and make up hand motions or a dance. (Song can be found online.)

Making God Famous

I. The Children's Workbook *(page 3, 4)*:

> **Discuss** the Reflection Question in *The Children's Workbook* for Week 1: Day 2 and have them write down their answer.

Look at the Cat and Dog Cartoon and fill in a possible response for the cat and dog. (There is no right or wrong answer.) You'll find the actual cartoon on page 2 in the cartoon book. You may want to look this up to guide your child's possible answer.

> While your child is coloring in the cartoon, discuss the difference between seeking to make God famous and asking God to make us famous. Make sure you emphasize the differences between being God-centered and self-centered in our Christianity.

II. I Heard Good News Today 2: Big Life:

- Find the country of **Iran** on a globe or the map in *I Heard Good News Today 2: Big Life* on page IX.
- Read Chapter 1, **"The Imam,"** in *I Heard Good News Today 2: Big Life* beginning on page 1.

III. The Children's Workbook:

> **Discuss:** How did Mr. Heerema make God famous by his attitudes or actions?

Pray for missionaries to be sent to the 77 million people in Iran.

IV. Optional Cartoon:

Look up Cartoon #33 in the cartoon book and discuss different reactions to a very hot day.

Making God Famous

I. The Children's Workbook *(page 5, 6)*:

> ***Discuss*** the Reflection Question in *The Children's Workbook* on page 5.
> Have them write their answer down in the space provided.

Look at the Cat and Dog Cartoon and talk about how Cats and Dogs are loved equally by God. God's love for us is not dependent upon what we do. God loves us because God is love. It has nothing to do with us. It simply is who God is! The cartoon can be found on page 1 in the cartoon book.

> While your child is coloring in the cartoon, ***discuss*** how you love your child unconditionally.

II. I Heard Good News Today 2: Big Life:

- Find the country of ***India*** on a globe or the map in I Heard Good News Today 2: Big Life page VII.
- Read Chapter 2, "**Frustrated in India**," in *I Heard Good News Today 2: Big Life* on page 5.

III. The Children's Workbook:

> ***Discuss*** how the main character made God famous and have them write it down in the workbook.

Pray for missionaries to be sent to the 1.25 billion people in India.

IV. Optional Cartoon:

Look up Cartoon #74 in the cartoon book and discuss what they should do when offered to watch an R Rated movie.

Week 2- Making God Famous Through Nature

I. Teaching:

Close your eyes and imagine the most beautiful place on earth.

> *Discuss:* What do you see there? Feel? Smell? Hear?
>
> Did you see a beautiful ocean and hear the waves? Did you see a field of colorful flowers and smell a sweet aroma? Did you see huge mountains covered in snow and feel the cold wind?

All of nature, in its different sizes and shapes and colors, is also there to make God famous—and we get to enjoy it too!

Read Romans 11:36, "For from him and through him and for him are all things. To him be the glory forever! Amen."

Note that it doesn't say, "So **some things** are from and through and for God." Nor does it say, "**Most things** are from and through and for God?" And it doesn't say, "**Only nice things** are from and through and for God."

> *Discuss:* What does the verse say? **(All things!)**

Yes, all things were designed to point us to God because they came from him and are for him. All things are on the earth to make God famous.

> *Discuss:* So a tree should make God famous, right? And birds? And grass? A house? A car? The beach? Clouds?

Yes, all things.

> *Discuss:* What else can you think of that is designed to make God famous?

The list is endless! One way nature points us to God is by praising him, only most of the time we don't realize it. Did you know that when a bird sings or a tree claps its leaves, it's praising God? To imagine this, have your mom turn on the audio CD and listen to me explaining it to you in person! And then try to make your own sounds of how nature is glorifying God.

All of nature was designed to make God famous, and when we praise God we are joining in the praise of the world around us.

II. Memory Verse:

Our memory verse for this week is Colossians 1:16b, "...all things have been created through him and for him."

III. Theme Song:

Play Track 1 on the Cat and Dog Audio CD provided in this kit. Have your kids sing along with our curriculum theme song, "We Want To Make God Famous!" See page 196 for the words.

IV. Prayer to Go:

Discuss verse with your child and conclude today's teaching with praying Prayer to Go #8, praising God as the creator of all things. (You can either listen to it on the internet or pray the words below.)

"All things were created by him and for him." Colossians 1:16

Dear Lord, I praise and worship You because You are the Creator of all things and these things show Your glory. May I remember to give You praise each time I see part of Your beautiful creation.

V. The Children's Workbook *(page 7, 8)*:

To finish the day, have your child open to Week 2: Day 1 in the Cat & Dog Children's Workbook. Students will write out the weekly verse. Have them complete the "God's Joy In Nature" activity page.

VI. Optional Activity:

If possible, go outside and spend 10 minutes enjoying the nature around you, looking and listening with new eyes and ears. If not possible, go to www.nationalgeographic.com and explore many beautiful photos and videos of nature, praising God for His creativity.

Making God Famous Through Nature

I. Because He Liked It!:

To begin, open the book *Because He Liked It!* and read a few examples of how nature makes God famous just by showing off His creative designs!

II. The Children's Workbook *(page 9, 10)*:

> **Discuss** the Reflection Question in *The Children's Workbook* on page 9. Have them write their answer down in the space provided.

Then, look at the Cat and Dog Cartoon and fill in a possible response for the cat and dog. (There is no right or wrong answer.) You'll find the actual cartoon on page 29 in the cartoon book. You may want to look this up to guide your child's answer.

> While your child is coloring in the cartoon, **discuss** how you can see God's glory in nature.

III. I Heard Good News Today 2: Big Life:

- Find the country of **India** on a globe or the map in I Heard Good News Today 2: Big Life page VII.
- Read Chapter 3, "**The Empty Hole**," in *I Heard Good News Today 2: Big Life* on page 9.

IV. The Children's Workbook:

> **Discuss**: Who made God famous by their attitudes or actions and how did they do it?

Pray for missionaries to be sent to the 997 million Hindus of India.

V. Optional Cartoon:

Look up Cartoon #4 in *Because He Liked It!* and learn what makes an elephant special!

Making God Famous Through Nature

I. The Children's Workbook *(page 11, 12)*:

> **Discuss** the Reflection Question in *The Children's Workbook* on page 11. Have them write their answer down in the space provided.

Then, look at the Cat and Dog Cartoon and fill in a possible response for the cat and dog. (There is no right or wrong answer.) You'll find the actual cartoon on page 4 in the cartoon book. You may want to look this up to guide your child's possible answer.

> While your child is coloring in the cartoon, discuss glorifying God when watching a sunset.

II. I Heard Good News Today 2: Big Life:

- Find the country of **India** on a globe or the map in I Heard Good News Today 2: Big Life page VII.
- Read Chapter 4, "**Crushed Dreams Brought Back To Life**," in *I Heard Good News Today 2: Big Life* on page 11.

III. The Children's Workbook:

> **Discuss**: Who made God famous by their attitudes or actions and how did they do it?

Pray for the 2% Christians (25 million) of India to be strong in their faith and to reach out to the Muslims and Hindus of their country. (Don't forget to review the memory verse!)

IV. Optional Cartoon:

Look up Cartoon #18 in *Because He Liked It!* and learn why only birds can fly!

Week 3- Making God Famous Through a Servant Attitude

I. Teaching:

> **Discuss:** What does it mean to serve someone? How many of you like to be served?

It's often really nice to have someone serve us a meal, drive us around, volunteer to help us clean our room or work on school—and the great thing is that we can also do that for others. Jesus showed us that one very powerful way to make God famous is to serve others. In fact, the Bible tells us that Jesus came not to be served, but to serve! He came to give his life for us (Mark 10:45). We are called to follow the path of Jesus.

But many times that is hard. Although we like being served, we don't always like to serve.

> **Discuss:** Do you like volunteering to do extra chores? Do you enjoy watching your younger siblings to help your mom? Do you always offer to help when you notice someone is having trouble?

Although Jesus showed us the straight path to pleasing God, it's not always easy for us to follow. We often act like Cats, who just want to be served. But the more we know about making God look good, the more we can ask his help to live in such a way.

Let's imagine a child is asked by his mom to set the table for dinner. He is playing outside and doesn't want to come in. So when she asks, he yells, "In a minute!" but keeps playing for five minutes and she has to ask again. This time he again says, "Just a minute!" but still doesn't come in.

> **Discuss:** Is the little boy acting like a Cat or a Dog? How so? Did he make God look good? How else could he respond?

Or imagine a little girl who noticed her mom folding lots of sheets and towels in the living room? Although she, too, was playing outside and wasn't asked to help, when she noticed her mom with lots to do, she came in and offered to help.

> **Discuss:** Is the girl acting like a Cat or a Dog? How so? Did she make God look good by her actions?

Jesus showed us that we can make God famous by serving others. In fact, we should seek to serve more than be served. He modeled that way of living.

II. *Memory Verse:*

Our memory verse for this week is Mark 10:45, "For even the Son of Man did not come to be served, but to serve, and to give his life as a ransom for many."

> *Discuss:* Talk about what the verse means with your child.

III. *Theme Song:*

Play Track 1 on the Cat and Dog Audio CD provided in this kit. Have your kids sing along with our curriculum theme song, "We Want To Make God Famous!" See page 196 for the words.

IV. *Prayer to Go:*

Conclude today's teaching with praying Prayer to Go #32, asking God to help us have a servant attitude. (You can either listen to it on the internet or pray the words below.)

"For even the Son of Man did not come to be served, but to serve." Mark 10:45

Help me remember that since Jesus came to serve and not be served—that should be my attitude also. Open my eyes to ways I can serve others for Your glory every day.

V. *The Children's Workbook* (page 13, 14)*:*

To finish the day, have your child open to Week 3: Day 1 in the Cat & Dog Children's Workbook. Students will write out the weekly verse and complete the "Match the Miracles" activity page. The matches are to the right:

VI. *Optional Activity:*

Act out a story of Jesus serving others, like washing his disciples' feet, healing many sick, feeding the hungry... (Scripture references are found on this week's activity sheet in *The Children's Workbook*.)

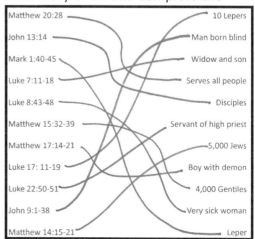

Matthew 20:28	10 Lepers
John 13:14	Man born blind
Mark 1:40-45	Widow and son
Luke 7:11-18	Serves all people
Luke 8:43-48	Disciples
Matthew 15:32-39	Servant of high priest
Matthew 17:14-21	5,000 Jews
Luke 17: 11-19	Boy with demon
Luke 22:50-51	4,000 Gentiles
John 9:1-38	Very sick woman
Matthew 14:15-21	Leper

Making God Famous Through
a Servant Attitude

I. The Children's Workbook *(page 15, 16)*:

> ***Discuss*** the Reflection Question in *The Children's Workbook* for Week 3: Day 2 and have them write down their answer.

Then, look at the Cat and Dog Cartoon and fill in a possible response for the cat and dog. (There is no right or wrong answer.) You'll find the actual cartoon on page 7 in the cartoon book. You may want to look this up to guide your child's possible answer.

> While your child is coloring in the cartoon, ***discuss*** what it would look like for them to have a servant's attitude.

II. I Heard Good News Today 2: Big Life:

- Find the country of **India** on a globe or the map in *I Heard Good News Today 2: Big Life* page VII.
- Read Chapter 5, "**Works Prepared In Advance**," in *I Heard Good News Today 2: Big Life* on page 15.

III. The Children's Workbook:

> ***Discuss***: How did Isaac hurt God's reputation? Then what did he do to make God famous?

Pray for missionaries to be sent to the 125 million Muslims in that country. (Don't forget to review the memory verse!)

IV. Optional Cartoon:

Look up Cartoon #85 in the cartoon book and discuss how to respond when you're tempted to be jealous.

Making God Famous Through a Servant Attitude

I. The Children's Workbook *(page 17, 18)*:

> **Discuss** the Reflection Question in *The Children's Workbook* for Week 3: Day 3 and have them write down their answer.

Then, look at the Cat and Dog Cartoon and fill in a possible response for the cat and dog. (There is no right or wrong answer.) You'll find the actual cartoon on page 12 in the cartoon book. You may want to look this up to guide your child's possible answer.

> While your child is coloring in the cartoon, discuss glorifying God through service.

II. I Heard Good News Today 2: Big Life:

- Find the country of **India** on a globe or the map in *I Heard Good News Today 2: Big Life* on page IX.
- Read Chapter 6, **"The Overdose,"** in *I Heard Good News Today 2: Big Life* beginning on page 17.

III. The Children's Workbook:

> **Discuss:** How did Rupesh make God famous by his attitudes or actions?

Pray for missionaries to be sent to the 57,000 Chamar (Pahari) Hindus of Northern India. (Don't forget to review the memory verse!)

IV. Optional Cartoon:

Optional Cartoon: Look up Cartoon #29 in *Because He Liked It!* and learn what is so funny about hamsters.

Week 4- Making God Famous Through Obeying My Parents

I. Teaching:

> *Discuss:* What did we learn from Jesus last week about making God famous? What did He model for us?

Yes, Jesus showed us that we can make God famous by serving others—He didn't come down to be served but to serve! Well, Jesus showed us something else: we can make God famous by obeying our parents. In fact, Jesus told us that He only spoke what His Father told Him to speak, and He only did the will of His Father (Look up John 12:49-50).

In Ephesians, children are commanded to obey their parents in the Lord, and are told it is the first commandment with a promise—that you may enjoy long life on earth! (Ephesians 6:1-3). So a Dog knows it pleases God and makes Him look good when children obey their parents.

So let's imagine a child's parents asked her not to watch a certain show because it does not model behavior that honors God. When the girl is at her friend's house, however, the friend turns on the show. Perhaps the friend even knows the other girl isn't supposed to watch it. What are her options?

> *Discuss:* What would be a Dog's response? What about a Cat? Which would make God famous?

Or what about a little boy who is supposed to stay quiet while visiting some family friends. His parents asked him to listen quietly while the family shares about their trip overseas, but it's boring to him and he just wants to go play. He knows what his parents want him to do, however, so he chooses to obey and sits quietly until they are finished, even though he was quite bored.

> *Discuss:* Was the boy acting like a Cat or Dog? Did his actions make God look good to his parents and the other family?

God has made it clear that it honors Him and makes Him famous when children obey their parents respectfully. This is one way to act like a Dog.

II. *Memory Verse:*

Our memory verse for this week is Ephesians 6:1, "Children, obey your parents in the Lord, for this is right."

> *Discuss:* Talk about what the verse means with your child.

III. *Theme Song:*

Play Track 1 on the Cat and Dog Audio CD provided in this kit. Have your kids sing along with our curriculum theme song, "We Want To Make God Famous!" See page 196 for the words.

IV. *Prayer to Go:*

Conclude today's teaching with praying Prayer to Go #29, asking God to help us obey our parents.

> "Children, obey your parents in the Lord, for this is right. Honor Your father and mother." Ephesians 6:1,2

> *Dear Lord, I don't always show love and honor to my parents the way I should. Help me obey them and give them respect because this is right and pleases You.*

V. *The Children's Workbook* (page 19, 20):

To finish the day, have your child open to Week 4: Day 1 in their *Children's Workbook*. Students will write out the weekly verse and complete the "Shapes Code" activity page. **(Answer: "Honor your father and mother"—this is the first commandment with a promise: "so that it may be well with you and you may live long on the earth.")**

VI. *Optional Activity:*

Play Simon Says to practice quick obedience!

Making God Famous Through obeying My Parents

I. The Children's Workbook (page 21, 22):

> **Discuss** the Reflection Question in *The Children's Workbook* for Week 4: Day 2 and have them write down their answer.

Then, look at the Cat and Dog Cartoon and fill in a possible response for the cat and dog. (There is no right or wrong answer.) You'll find the actual cartoon on page 8 in the cartoon book. You may want to look this up to guide your child's possible answer.

> While your child is coloring in the cartoon, **discuss** following directions quickly.

II. I Heard Good News Today 2: Big Life:

- Find the country of **India** on a globe or the map in *I Heard Good News Today 2: Big Life* on page IX. (If it is getting too easy, go to page 181 of *The Children's Workbook*.)
- Read Chapter 7, **"Playing The Perfect Role,"** in *I Heard Good News Today 2: Big Life* beginning on page 19.

III. The Children's Workbook:

> **Discuss**: What did Suman know at the end of the story that made God famous?

Pray for missionaries to be sent to the 1.4 million Adi Dharmi Hindus of India. (Don't forget to review the memory verse!)

IV. Optional Cartoon:

Look up Cartoon #75 in the cartoon book and discuss using free time when no parents are watching.

Making God Famous Through obeying My Parents

I. The Children's Workbook (page 23, 24):

> **Discuss** the Reflection Question in *The Children's Workbook* for Week 4: Day 3 and have them write down their answer.

Then, look at the Cat and Dog Cartoon and fill in a possible response for the cat and dog. (There is no right or wrong answer.) You'll find the actual cartoon on page 18 in the cartoon book. You may want to look this up to guide your child's possible answer.

> While your child is coloring in the cartoon, **discuss** how it can sometimes be hard to obey our parents—yet we still need to do it.

II. I Heard Good News Today 2: Big Life:

- Find the country of **India** on a globe or the map in *I Heard Good News Today 2: Big Life* on page IX.
- Read Chapter 8, **"A Failed Test,"** in *I Heard Good News Today 2: Big Life* beginning on page 23.

III. The Children's Workbook:

> **Discuss:** What did Dharmendra do to make God look bad and then look good?

Pray for missionaries to be sent to the 1.2 million Banjara Hindus in that country. (Don't forget to review the memory verse!)

IV. Optional Cartoon:

Look up Cartoon #72 in the cartoon book and discuss showing respect to parents when they've driven you somewhere.

Week 5- Making God Famous Through Respecting Other Adults

I. Teaching:

Who likes having grandparents or aunts and uncles come and visit?

Did you know that just as it glorifies God when we obey our parents, it also makes him famous when we obey and respect other adults? These could be family members, teachers, or even family friends. Let's consider an example.

What if a new family comes over for dinner at your house, someone you've never met. They enter the door and your parents ask you to come say hello. You're really shy, however, and do not like saying hello to people you don't know, so you just hide behind your dad and don't say anything.

> *Discuss:* Were you acting like a Dog, thinking of others and pleasing God? Or were you acting like a Cat, thinking only of yourself? How could you have acted like a Dog?

Or what if you're at basketball practice, and the coach is trying to teach a new skill. You're sitting by your best friend, however, and keep trying to make him/her laugh. Your coach is getting frustrated that you're not paying attention and keeps asking you to be quiet.

> *Discuss:* Was talking while the coach was talking showing respect? Did that make God famous? Were you thinking more about yourself or the coach and the team?
>
> What are some other times you interact with other adults and have a chance to show respect? What actions could make God famous?

II. Memory Verse:

Our memory verse for this week is 1 Samuel 15:22b, "To obey is better than sacrifice."

> *Discuss:* Talk about what this verse means with your child.

III. Theme Song:

Play Track 1 on the Cat and Dog Audio CD provided in this kit. Have your kids sing along with our curriculum theme song, "We Want To Make God Famous!" See page 196 for the words.

IV. Prayer to Go:

Conclude today's teaching with praying Prayer to Go #16, asking God to help us obey because it brings Him glory.

"To obey is better than sacrifice." 1 Samuel 15:22b

Dear Lord, I want to obey You because this gives You glory. Keep me from going my own way.

V. The Children's Workbook *(page 25, 26)*:

To finish the day, have your child open to Week 5: Day 1 in *The Children's Workbook*. Have your student write out the weekly verse and complete the "Word Cluster" activity page. **(Possible answers: Obey, Help, Listen To, Be Thankful, Do Chores, Love Them, Love Siblings, Look Them In The Eye, Shake Their Hand, Don't Interrupt, etc.)**

VI. Optional Activity:

Role-play different scenarios of showing respect to adults. Let the children pretend to be the adults with you responding like the child. Reverse the roles and do it again!

Making God Famous Through
Respecting Other Adults

I. The Children's Workbook (page 27, 28):

> **Discuss** the Reflection Question in *The Children's Workbook* for Week 5: Day 2 and have them write down their answer.

Then, look at the Cat and Dog Cartoon and fill in a possible response for the cat and the dog. (There is no right or wrong answer.) You'll find the actual cartoon on page 82 in the cartoon book. You may want to look this up to guide your child's possible answer.

> While your child is coloring in the cartoon, **discuss** respecting other adults at church on Sunday mornings.

II. I Heard Good News Today 2: Big Life:

- Find the country of **India** on a globe or the map in *I Heard Good News Today 2: Big Life* on page IX.
- Read Chapter 9, **"The Boy With No Voice,"** in *I Heard Good News Today 2: Big Life* beginning on page 25.

III. The Children's Workbook:

> **Discuss**: How did Kuldeep make God famous by his attitudes or actions?

Pray for missionaries to be sent to the 27 million Maharata Hindus in India. (Don't forget to review the memory verse!)

IV. Optional Cartoon:

Look up Cartoon #36 in the cartoon book and discuss respecting adults in charge when at a museum or library or other public place.

Making God Famous Through Respecting other Adults

I. The Children's Workbook (page 29, 30):

> ***Discuss*** the Reflection Question in *The Children's Workbook* for Week 5: Day 3 and have them write down their answer.

Then, look at the Cat and Dog Cartoon and fill in a possible response for the cat and the dog. (There is no right or wrong answer.) You'll find the actual cartoon on page 24 in the cartoon book. You may want to look this up to guide your child's possible answer.

> While your child is coloring in the cartoon, ***discuss*** showing respect even when an adult makes a decision you don't like.

II. *I Heard Good News Today 2: Big Life:*

- Find the country of ***Bangladesh*** on a globe or the map in *I Heard Good News Today 2: Big Life* on page IX.
- Read Chapter 10, **"Isa The Savior,"** in *I Heard Good News Today 2: Big Life* beginning on page 27.

III. The Children's Workbook:

> ***Discuss:*** How did Saifel make God famous by his attitudes or actions?

Pray for missionaries to be sent to the 191 million people of Bangladesh. (Don't forget to review the memory verse!)

IV. Optional Cartoon:

Look up the second Bonus Cartoon (page 105 in the cartoon book) and discuss what it means to share something that is precious to you.

Week 6– Making God Famous Through Loving Siblings

I. Teaching:

> *Discuss:* What is something you like about your brother or sister? What is something they do that you don't like so much? (If your child has no siblings, talk about friends in this lesson.)
>
> Do you think there are some things we do that God doesn't like? What could those be?

God is amazing! He never stops loving us and doing good to us, even when we do things He doesn't like. In fact, the Bible tells us that God is love! And it makes Him famous when we love others, especially our brothers and sisters. But we don't always do that. Let's think through some scenarios.

> So what if your little brother comes over to you and hits you (and you are so mad—because hitting is wrong and hurts) and you hit him back.
>
> Did that honor God? Did that make Him look good to your little brother or your family? Was that acting like a Cat or a Dog?
>
> ~~~~
>
> Or what if your older sister doesn't share her new markers with you, but when you get new crayons the next week, you still share with her because you know God wants us to share.
>
> Were your actions pleasing to God? To whom did they make God famous?
>
> ~~~~
>
> Maybe your sister is a little chubbier than you, and you and your siblings tease her about needing to go to "fat camp" or being "family" with the whales. You're just joking and it makes everyone laugh, so you don't feel bad about it.
>
> How would you feel, though, if someone said that about you? Do you think your teasing pleases God? Is that showing love to your sister?

It's not easy to love others like God loves us –especially our siblings! And yet that is a great way to make God famous. He delights when we are kind to others and think of their feelings, even when they don't do the same to us.

> **Discuss:** What is one way you can show love to your brother or sister today?

II. Memory Verse:

Our verse for this week is 1 John 4:21, "And he has given us this command: Anyone who loves God must also love their brother and sister."

> Discuss what this verse means with your child.

III. Theme Song:

Play Track 1 on the Cat and Dog Audio CD provided in this kit. Have your kids sing along with our curriculum theme song, "We Want To Make God Famous!" See page 196 for the words.

IV. Prayer to Go:

Conclude today's teaching with praying Prayer to Go #10, thanking God for his love.

"God is love." John 4:16

Dear Lord, Your love is so great I cannot understand it and do not deserve it. I love you, O Lord, my strength. Thank you for Your love that never ends.

V. The Children's Workbook *(page 31, 32)*:

To finish the day, have your child open to Week 6: Day 1 in *The Children's Workbook*. Have them write out the weekly verse and complete the "Draw Your Family" activity page.

VI. Optional Activity:

Either draw and color or print pictures of a cat and a dog. Cut them out and display somewhere around the house to remind you to live like a Dog!

Making God Famous Through
Loving Siblings

I. The Children's Workbook (page 33, 34):

> **Discuss** the Reflection Question in *The Children's Workbook* for Week 6: Day 2 and have them write down their answer.

Then, look at the Cat and Dog Cartoon and fill in a possible response for the cat and the dog. (There is no right or wrong answer.) You'll find the actual cartoon on page 47 in the cartoon book. You may want to look this up to guide your child's possible answer.

> While your child is coloring in the cartoon, **discuss** showing love when your little sibling or a friend is crying.

II. I Heard Good News Today 2: Big Life:

- Find the country of **India** on a globe or the map in *I Heard Good News Today 2: Big Life* on page IX.
- Read Chapter 11, **"The Perfect Rest,"** in *I Heard Good News Today 2: Big Life* beginning on page 29.

III. The Children's Workbook:

> **Discuss:** Have your student write three events in the story that led to making God famous!

Pray for missionaries to be sent to the 1 million Banajiga Hindus in India. (Don't forget to review the memory verse!)

IV. Optional Cartoon:

Look up Cartoon #19 in *Because He Liked It!* and learn about birds that run on water to fly!

Makiñg Gọd Famọus Through
Lọ̈Viñg Sibliñgs

I. The Children's Workbook (page 35, 36):

> **Discuss** the Reflection Question in *The Children's Workbook* for Week 6: Day 3 and have them write down their answer.

Then, look at the Cat and Dog Cartoon and fill in a possible response for the cat and the dog. (There is no right or wrong answer.) You'll find the actual cartoon on page 28 in the cartoon book. You may want to look this up to guide your child's possible answer.

> While your child is coloring in the cartoon, **discuss** what to do when they want a toy someone else is playing with.

II. I Heard Good News Today 2: Big Life:

- Find the country of **Nepal** on a globe or the map in *I Heard Good News Today 2: Big Life* on page IX.
- Read Chapter 12, **"You're Finished,"** in *I Heard Good News Today 2: Big Life* beginning on page 33.

III. The Children's Workbook:

> **Discuss:** What miracle did God do to make Himself famous in Sanjay's eyes?

Pray for missionaries to be sent to the 3.3 million Brahman Hindus of Nepal. (Don't forget to review the memory verse!)

IV. Optional Cartoon:

Look up Cartoon #100 in the cartoon book and discuss being willing to forgive someone who has hurt you or done an injustice to you.

Week 7- Making God Famous Through Loving others

I. Teaching:

> How many commands do you think are in the Bible? Do you know which is the most important one?

When someone asked Jesus what was the greatest command, He answered in two parts: Love the Lord your God and love your neighbor as yourself. Loving others is what we're called to do! And one of the best ways to love others is to treat them like we want to be treated. This can be hard to do, but if we stop and think about our actions and words before we speak and act, we can make choices that please God. A Dog is concerned with making God look good no matter who he or she is around.

> What if, for example, you are with a group of kids and you don't know very many of them because you're new. Everyone is sitting in groups to eat their snack and you don't know where to sit.
>
> How would you feel in this moment? What could someone do that would make you feel better?
>
> ~~~~~
>
> Well, what if a few months later you're with another group, and this time you have many friends. You are all sitting down to eat and you notice a new kid who is sitting by himself. You don't really want to invite him to sit with you because you've never met him before, and who knows what the other kids will say, but all of a sudden you think—what would make God famous?
>
> What did you want to happen, when you were in the same situation as this new kid? What could you do that would make God look famous?

It's always a good idea to think before you speak or act, and now you have two helpful questions to ask yourself:

1. How would I want to be treated?
2. And what would make God look good?

II. Memory Verse:

Our verse for this week is 1 John 4:11, "Dear friends, since God so loved us, we also ought to love one another."

> ***Discuss*** what this verse means with your child.

III. Theme Song:

Play Track 1 on the Cat and Dog Audio CD provided in this kit. Have your kids sing along with our curriculum theme song, "We Want To Make God Famous!" See page 196 for the words.

IV. Prayer to Go:

Conclude today's teaching with praying Prayer to Go #19, asking God to help us love others.

"Whoever loves God must also love his brother." 1 John 4:21

Dear Lord, help me love others with the same love You have given to me.

V. The Children's Workbook *(page 37, 38)*:

To finish the day, have your child open to Week 7: Day 1 in *The Children's Workbook*. Have your student write out the weekly verse and complete the "Tic-Tac-Toe Code" activity page.

VI. Optional Activity:

Make a card for someone who needs encouragement, reminding them how much they are loved. Deliver it in person or send it through the mail!

Making God famous Through
Loving others

I. The Children's Workbook *(page 39, 40)*:

> ***Discuss*** the Reflection Question in *The Children's Workbook* for Week 7: Day 2 and have them write down their answer.

Then, look at the Cat and Dog Cartoon and fill in a possible response for the cat and dog. (There is no right or wrong answer.) You'll find the actual cartoon on page 49 in the cartoon book. You may want to look this up to guide your child's possible answer.

> While your child is coloring in the cartoon, ***discuss*** respecting the baby-sitter.

II. *I Heard Good News Today 2: Big Life:*

* Find the country of ***India*** on a globe or the map in *I Heard Good News Today 2: Big Life* on page IX.
* Read Chapter 13, **"The Evil Spirit,"** in *I Heard Good News Today 2: Big Life* beginning on page 35.

III. The Children's Workbook:

> ***Discuss:*** List three things that God used to make Himself famous in Shantanus' eyes.

Pray for missionaries to be sent to the 12 million Ansari-Momin Muslims of India. (Don't forget to review the memory verse!)

IV. Optional Cartoon:

Look up Cartoon #78 in the cartoon book and discuss what to do if you accidentally hit someone while playing a game.

Making God Famous Through Loving others

I. *The Children's Workbook* (page 41, 42)*:*

> ***Discuss*** the Reflection Question in *The Children's Workbook* for Week 7: Day 3 and have them write down their answer.

Then, look at the Cat and Dog Cartoon and fill in a possible response for the cat and dog. (There is no right or wrong answer.) You'll find the actual cartoon on page 20 in the cartoon book. You may want to look this up to guide your child's possible answer.

> While your child is coloring in the cartoon, ***discuss*** treating others fairly when playing games.

II. *I Heard Good News Today 2: Big Life:*

- Find the country of **Nepal** on a globe or the map in *I Heard Good News Today 2: Big Life* on page IX.
- Read Chapter 14, **"A Gift For His Son,"** in *I Heard Good News Today 2: Big Life* beginning on page 39.

III. *The Children's Workbook:*

> ***Discuss:*** How did Bishal and his father make God famous by their attitudes or actions?

Pray for missionaries to be sent to the 1.4 million Tharu Hindus of Nepal. (Don't forget to review the memory verse!)

IV. *Optional Cartoon:*

Look up Cartoon #34 in the cartoon book and discuss having good sportsmanship even when playing in the backyard.

Week 8- Making God Famous
Through Doing Chores

I. Teaching:

> *Discuss:* What is your favorite chore to do? What is your least favorite chore?

Did you know God cares about the way we do our chores? In fact, He's told us that no matter what we are doing, we should do our best since we're doing it for Him. So whether we're doing schoolwork, taking care of our dog, making our bed, setting the table, or taking out the trash, we should do it as if we're working for God, not just our parents or teachers.

> *Discuss:* So how would you make your bed as if you were making it for God? How would that be different if you were just doing it for yourself?

Suppose a child has a responsibility to clean her room. When she cleans it, however, she doesn't actually clean it well. Instead, she stuffs everything into the closet and under the bed. Her toys and markers are all jumbled together and none of the socks are matched. It may look clean when someone first walks into the room, but if she tried to get anything out, the mess would be revealed.

> *Discuss:* How does that make God look? Do you think He would be pleased with a "half-hearted" job? Does that seem like a Cat or Dog's way of cleaning a room?

Or suppose a boy has a responsibility to take care of his dog. It's his job to feed her every morning and play with her outside every afternoon. At first, it was really fun for him to take care of his puppy. But as the months went by, it started to be less fun and more work. Sometimes, in the afternoon, he just wanted to stay inside and play his own games instead of taking her outside. But, he chose to fulfill his responsibility anyway because that was his job and his dog was counting on him. Plus, God wants us to take care of His creation and do our best. So the boy always made a little time to take his dog outside and tried to have a good attitude.

> *Discuss:* How does his commitment make God look? Is God pleased with his actions?
>
> What is a chore you have to do that you could choose to do a little better, completing it as if for God?

II. Memory Verse:

Our memory verse for this week is Colossians 3:23, "Whatever you do, work at it with all your heart, as working for the Lord, not for men..."

> ***Discuss** what the verse means with your child.*

III. Theme Song:

Play Track 1 on the Cat and Dog Audio CD provided in this kit. Have your kids sing along with Miss Elise's class in the Middle East and then other elementary kids from Richmond. Then do verse 3 on your own! See page 196 for the words.

IV. Prayer to Go:

Conclude today's teaching with praying Prayer to Go #35, asking God to help us do our work well.

"Whatever you do, do it with all your heart, as working for the Lord, not men." Colossians 3:23

Dear Lord, when I have work to do at home or in school, may I do it well. Let my work bring glory to Your name.

V. The Children's Workbook *(page 43, 44)*:

To finish the day, have your child open to Week 8: Day 1 in *The Children's Workbook*. Have your student write out the weekly verse and complete the "Hidden Chores" activity page. (The key is to the right.)

VI. Optional Activity:

Mess up the covers and pillows on your bed or a sibling's bed (with their permission), then, have a race to see who can make the other's bed or your own look good for God today!

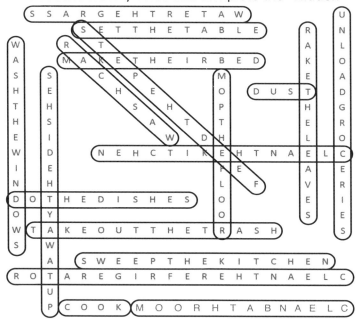

Making God Famous
Through Doing Chores

I. The Children's Workbook (page 45, 46):

> **Discuss** the Reflection Question in *The Children's Workbook* for Week 8: Day 2 and have them write down their answer.

Then, look at the Cat and Dog Cartoon and fill in a possible response for the cat and dog. (There is no right or wrong answer.) You'll find the actual cartoon on page 16 in the cartoon book. You may want to look this up to guide your child's possible answer.

> While your child is coloring in the cartoon, **discuss** making your bed as if for God.

II. I Heard Good News Today 2: Big Life:

- Find the country of **Afghanistan** on a globe or the map in *I Heard Good News Today 2: Big Life* on page IX.
- Read Chapter 15, **"The Man on the White Horse,"** in *I Heard Good News Today 2: Big Life* beginning on page 41.

III. The Children's Workbook:

> **Discuss:** How did Sadeq make God famous by his attitudes or actions?

Pray for missionaries to be sent to the 9 million Northern Pakthun Muslims of Afghanistan. (Don't forget to review the memory verse!)

IV. Optional Cartoon:

Look up Cartoon #22 in *Because He Liked It!* and learn what the eagle uses to hunt its favorite food.

Making God Famous
Through Doing Chores

I. *The Children's Workbook* (page 47, 48):

> ***Discuss*** the Reflection Question in *The Children's Workbook* for Week 8: Day 3 and have them write down their answer.

Then, look at the Cat and Dog Cartoon and fill in a possible response for the cat and dog. (There is no right or wrong answer.) You'll find the actual cartoon on page 10 in the cartoon book. You may want to look this up to guide your child's possible answer.

> While your child is coloring in the cartoon, ***discuss*** taking care of pets. How would a Dog do it? How would a Cat do it?

II. *I Heard Good News Today 2: Big Life:*

- Find the country of **Pakistan** on a globe or the map in *I Heard Good News Today 2: Big Life* on page IX.
- Read Chapter 16, **"The Carpenter,"** in *I Heard Good News Today 2: Big Life* beginning on page 43.

III. *The Children's Workbook:*

> ***Discuss*** How did Javid make God famous by this attitudes or actions?

Pray for missionaries to be sent to the 2.7 million Gujjar Muslims of Pakistan. (Don't forget to review the memory verse!)

IV. *Optional Cartoon:*

Go to cartoon #101 in *Because He Like It!* and see if you would want a tongue the size of a woodpecker's tongue!

Week 9- Making God Famous Through Wholeheartedly Serving God

I. Teaching:

How would you feel if Mom and Dad served you half a meal? Or what if you drove halfway to vacation and then stopped?

God tells us that whether we're eating or drinking, or whatever we're doing, we should do it all for the glory of God (1 Corinthians 10:31). Just like whatever chores we're doing should be done for God, this verse says whatever we do at all times should be done for Him!

> **Discuss:** Take out a sheet of paper and list all the things you do in a day. (Examples: eat, sleep, play, talk, ride in car, read, write, learn, walk, brush teeth, hug mom...)

All these things should be done in a way that pleases God and makes Him look good. Serving Him with all our heart and not just half way.

> **Discuss:** How would you feel if your mom or dad only gave you half hugs? How would your mom and dad feel if you only gave them half a hug? What would happen if you only brushed half your teeth your entire life?

We know that God has given us commands to love others and show respect. But often we only do it half the time.

> **Discuss:** How do you think God feels when we do half of what He asks us to do?

God is made famous when we serve him –no matter what we're doing—with our whole hearts.

II. Memory Verse:

Our memory verse for this week is 1 Corinthians 10:31, "So whether you eat or drink or whatever you do, do it all for the glory of God."

> **Discuss** what this verse means with your child.

III. Theme Song:

Play Track 1 on the Cat and Dog Audio CD provided in this kit. Have your kids sing along with our curriculum theme song, "We Want To Make God Famous!" See page 196 for the words.

IV. Prayer to Go:

Conclude today's teaching with praying Prayer to Go #5, asking God to help us be fully committed to Him.

"But your heart must be fully committed to the Lord Your God, to live by his decrees and obey his commands." 1 Kings 8:61 (NIV)

Dear Lord, I choose to be fully committed to You. I cannot do this on my own. I will need Your help as I learn to follow and grow in my obedience to You.

V. The Children's Workbook *(page 49, 50)*:

To finish the day, have your child open to Week 9: Day 1 in *The Children's Workbook*. Have your student write out the weekly verse and complete the "Wholehearted Activities" activity page. **(Answers by each line: My Chores / Feeding The Pet / Making My Bed / Cleaning My Room / Saying Please / Washing Dishes / Dusting / Helping Mom / Turning Off Lights / School Work / Loving God / Encouraging Others.)**

VI. Optional Activity:

Listen to tracks 10, 11 and 12 on the Cat and Dog Audio CD. Decide which choruses are "Catish" or "Dogish".

Please note that the word *tessera* is sung in one of the songs. A *tessera* is one piece of glass in a stained glass window. The idea behind the song is that creation around us is one big beautifully stained glass window that God wants to shine His glory through. And each bit has it's own unique way of revealing that glory. Hence the words, "Give us eyes to see each tessera You've ordained to sing your praise" is referencing a prayer to see the glory of God in nature—as well as in all areas of life—because we can be so busy, we often miss it.

Please note that not only can we think, "It's all about us," but we can think, "It's all about *things*." It could also be all about *power, prestige, homes, families, marriage, children,* etc. There are millions of ways we can fill in the blank of "It's all about _____." Each one can replace God and becomes an idol if we are not careful.

Making God Famous Through
Wholeheartedly Serving God

I. The Children's Workbook *(page 51, 52)*:

> **Discuss** the Reflection Question in *The Children's Workbook* for Week 9: Day 2 and have them write down their answer.

Then, look at the Cat and Dog Cartoon and fill in a possible response for the cat and dog. (There is no right or wrong answer.) You'll find the actual cartoon on page 14 in the cartoon book. You may want to look this up to guide your child's possible answer.

> While your child is coloring in the cartoon, **discuss** serving God even in small tasks.

II. I Heard Good News Today 2: Big Life:

- Find the country of **Afghanistan** on a globe or the map in *I Heard Good News Today 2: Big Life* on page IX.
- Read Chapter 17, **"Books in the Backseat,"** in *I Heard Good News Today 2: Big Life* beginning on page 47.

III. The Children's Workbook:

> **Discuss:** How did Ahmed's boss make God famous by his attitudes or actions?

Pray for missionaries to be sent to the 5 million Hazara Muslims of Afghanistan. (Don't forget to review the memory verse!)

IV. Optional Cartoon:

Look up Cartoon #19 in the cartoon book and review serving God when cleaning your room.

Making God Famous Through
Wholeheartedly Serving God

I. The Children's Workbook (page 53, 54):

> **Discuss** the Reflection Question in *The Children's Workbook* for Week 9: Day 3 and have them write down their answer.

Then, look at the Cat and Dog Cartoon and fill in a possible response for the cat and dog. (There is no right or wrong answer.) You'll find the actual cartoon on page 89 in the cartoon book. You may want to look this up to guide your child's possible answer.

> While your child is coloring in the cartoon, **discuss** doing homework for God. If a person doesn't do it for God, who could they be doing it for?

II. I Heard Good News Today 2: Big Life:

- Find the country of **Nepal** on a globe or the map in *I Heard Good News Today 2: Big Life* on page IX.
- Read Chapter 18, **"Kicked Out By His Own Father,"** in *I Heard Good News Today 2: Big Life* beginning on page 49.

III. The Children's Workbook:

> **Discuss:** How did Prem make God famous by his attitudes or actions?

Pray for missionaries to be sent to the 475,000 Tamang of Nepal. (Don't forget to review the memory verse!)

IV. Optional Cartoon:

Look up Cartoon #41 in the cartoon book and discuss how to respond when something valuable is stolen.

Week 10- Making God Famous Through Thinking of others First

I. Teaching:

Do you remember the best way to love others?

Treat them like we want to be treated. In order to do this, we have to be thinking about others and not just ourselves. That's hard to do! More than we realize, our thoughts are about ourselves.

> *Discuss:* Have you ever seen a group picture that you're in? Who do you usually look for first?

Our natural tendency is to think about ourselves. But Jesus tells us just the opposite! He tells us to think of others more than ourselves and even as more important than ourselves! (Look up and read Philippians 2: 3-4). He tells us we should look for what is best for them and not what is best for us.

A Dog knows this and tries to consider those around her. A Dog tries to think about how others feel and what would be good for them. But a Cat—who thinks life is all about her—only cares how she feels and what she wants.

> Suppose you are playing soccer with friends and one of them misses a goal that would have tied the score. Some of the players on your team get very upset and yell at the boy, saying he's no good at soccer. One person even pushes him. Instead of just thinking about yourself and being glad it wasn't you, you start to think about your friend.
>
> How do you think he feels? How would you feel if you had missed the goal and were treated that way? How could you treat him now that would please God?
>
> ~~~~
>
> Or what if you're at the park and are playing on your favorite part: the swings. You don't get to come to the park very often, so you're so happy to be swinging high and fast. While you're swinging, you notice a child standing around the swings. She looks like she wants a turn, but all the swings are full. You don't want to stop swinging (you were here first!), but you start to think about the girl standing there.

We can make God famous when we think of others first, before we think of ourselves, and then make choices to do what is good for the other person.

II. Memory Verse:

Our memory verse for this week is Luke 6:31, "Do to others as you would have them do to you."

Discuss what this verse means with your child.

III. Theme Song:

Play Track 1 on the Cat and Dog Audio CD provided in this kit. Have your kids sing along with our curriculum theme song, "We Want To Make God Famous!" See page 196 for the words.

IV. Prayer to Go:

Conclude today's teaching with praying Prayer to Go #13, asking God to help us apologize if we've hurt someone.

"Let the words of my mouth and the meditations of my heart be pleasing in Your sight." Psalm 19:14

Dear Lord, when I have hurt someone by my words or deeds, make me willing to quickly apologize and make things right before them and You.

V. The Children's Workbook (page 55, 56):

To finish the day, have your child open to Week 10: Day 1 in *The Children's Workbook.* Have your student write out the weekly verse and complete the "Scrambled Eggs Word" activity page. **(The answer is: Don't push your way to the front; don't sweet-talk your way to the top. Put yourself aside, and help others get ahead. Don't be obsessed with getting your own advantage. Forget yourselves long enough to lend a helping hand. Philippians 2:3-4 The Message)**

VI. Optional Activity:

Act out scenarios where someone is being teased or is upset, and the others have to stand up for them and encourage them.

Making God Famous Through
Thinking of Others First

I. The Children's Workbook (page 57, 58):

> **Discuss** the Reflection Question in *The Children's Workbook* for Week 10: Day 2 and have them write down their answer.

Then, look at the Cat and Dog Cartoon and fill in a possible response for the cat and dog. (There is no right or wrong answer.) You'll find the actual cartoon on page 97 in the cartoon book. You may want to look this up to guide your child's possible answer.

> While your child is coloring in the cartoon, **discuss** teasing others. When is it acceptable? When is it not acceptable?

II. I Heard Good News Today 2: Big Life:

- Find the country of **Cambodia** on a globe or the map in *I Heard Good News Today 2: Big Life* on page IX.
- Read Chapter 19, **"Our Way of Life has not Changed, But Our Lord Has,"** in *I Heard Good News Today 2: Big Life* beginning on page 51.

III. The Children's Workbook:

> **Discuss:** What did God use to make Himself famous and how did it work?

Pray for missionaries to be sent to the 12.7 million Kmer Buddhists of Cambodia. (Don't forget to review the memory verse!)

IV. Optional Cartoon:

Look up Cartoon #88 in the cartoon book and discuss encouraging others when playing sports.

Making God Famous Through Thinking of others first

I. *The Children's Workbook* (page 59, 60):

> ***Discuss*** the Reflection Question in *The Children's Workbook* for Week 10: Day 3 and have them write down their answer.

Then, look at the Cat and Dog Cartoon and fill in a possible response for the cat and dog. (There is no right or wrong answer.) You'll find the actual cartoon on page 77 in the cartoon book. You may want to look this up to guide your child's possible answer.

> While your child is coloring in the cartoon, ***discuss*** going to a friend's house when you are sick. What is good about it? What is not good about it?

II. *I Heard Good News Today 2: Big Life*:

- Find the country of **Cambodia** on a globe or the map in *I Heard Good News Today 2: Big Life* on page IX.
- Read Chapter 20, **"A Person of Peace,"** in *I Heard Good News Today 2: Big Life* beginning on page 53.

III. *The Children's Workbook:*

> ***Discuss:*** How did Benjamin and Tharaoth make God famous by their attitudes or actions?

Pray for missionaries to be sent to the 500,000 Western Cham Muslims in Cambodia. (Don't forget to review the memory verse!)

IV. *Optional Cartoon:*

Look up Cartoon #64 in the cartoon book and discuss being flexible when playing games.

Week 11- Making God Famous Through Honesty

I. Teaching:

Have you ever done something you wished you didn't do? Were you tempted to lie about it?

Sometimes, when we make a mistake, we want to pretend we didn't do it. We wished we hadn't done it, and we don't want to accept responsibility for our actions. But the Bible is clear that God does not like lying lips, so we will make Him famous when we choose honesty, both in our words and deeds.

Part of honesty is taking responsibility for your actions and "owning" the choices you make. If you're playing with your sibling and you get upset and hit him, take ownership of what you did. Don't lie (I didn't hit him!), blame others (He hit me first!), or make excuses (It wasn't very hard!). Be honest and accept the consequences of your actions.

The more you take ownership for your words and deeds, the more people can trust you and the more famous God will be.

> **Discuss:** What if you were playing at your neighbor's house, and your mom had asked you to come home by 5 PM. You were having so much fun you didn't want to leave and stopped looking at the clock, so you didn't end up coming home until 5:30 PM.
>
> What excuses could you make? How could you blame others? What would it look like to take responsibility for your mistake?

God is pleased when we choose honesty in all areas of our life. In Ephesians 6:14, He even tells us to wear a "belt of truth" to stand firm against temptation. Dogs know that we make God look good when we take responsibility for our choices.

II. Memory Verse:

Our memory verse for this week is Proverbs 12:22, "The LORD detests lying lips, but he delights in people who are trustworthy."

> **Discuss** what this verse means with your child.

III. Theme Song:

Play Track 1 on the Cat and Dog Audio CD provided in this kit. Have your kids sing along with our curriculum theme song, "We Want To Make God Famous!" See page 196 for the words.

IV. Prayer to Go:

Conclude today's teaching with praying Prayer to Go #15, asking God to keep us truthful and honest.

> "The Lord detests lying lips, but he delights in men who are truthful."
> Proverbs 12:22

> *Dear Lord, keep me truthful and honest. Let my life show Your truth. If I am tempted to lie, remind me of Your Word.*

V. The Children's Workbook *(page 61, 62)*:

To finish the day, have your child open to Week 11: Day 1 in The Children's Workbook. Have your student write out the weekly verse and complete the "Morse Code" activity page. **(The answer is: Then you will know the truth, and the truth will set you free. John 8:32)**

VI. Optional Activity:

Make a "belt of truth" to wear throughout the day, either with paper or whatever material you have around the house. Then, whenever someone is tempted to not tell the truth, discuss taking ownership. You can even go through all the options (lying, blaming others, making excuses) and then conclude with the truth.

Making God Famous Through Honesty

I. The Children's Workbook *(page 63, 64)*:

> ***Discuss*** the Reflection Question in *The Children's Workbook* for Week 11: Day 2 and have them write down their answer.

Then, look at the Cat and Dog Cartoon and fill in a possible response for the cat and dog. (There is no right or wrong answer.) You'll find the actual cartoon on page 48 in the cartoon book. You may want to look this up to guide your child's possible answer.

> While your child is coloring in the cartoon, ***discuss*** scenarios when your children might not want to tell the truth but must to honor God.

II. I Heard Good News Today 2: Big Life:

- Find the country of **Vietnam** on a globe or the map in *I Heard Good News Today 2: Big Life* on page IX.
- Read Chapter 21, **"The License,"** in *I Heard Good News Today 2: Big Life* beginning on page 55.

III. The Children's Workbook:

> ***Discuss:*** How did Deiu Sanh make God famous by his attitudes or actions?

Pray for missionaries to be sent to the 1.3 million Unreligious Hmong in Vietnam. (Don't forget to review the memory verse!)

IV. Optional Cartoon:

Look up Cartoon #20 in the cartoon book and discuss being honest when playing games.

Making God Famous Through Honesty

I. The Children's Workbook (page 65, 66):

> **Discuss** the Reflection Question in *The Children's Workbook* for Week 11: Day 3 and have them write down their answer.

Then, look at the Cat and Dog Cartoon and fill in a possible response for the cat and dog. (There is no right or wrong answer.) You'll find the actual cartoon on page 22 in the cartoon book. You may want to look this up to guide your child's possible answer.

> While your child is coloring in the cartoon, **discuss** what it means to take ownership of your actions.

II. I Heard Good News Today 2: Big Life:

- Find the country of **Pakistan** on a globe or the map in *I Heard Good News Today 2: Big Life* on page IX.
- Read Chapter 22, **"A Tiger for Jesus,"** in *I Heard Good News Today 2: Big Life* beginning on page 57.

III. The Children's Workbook:

> **Discuss:** How did Francis make God famous by his attitudes or actions?

Pray for missionaries to be sent to the 2.3 million Centra Pathan Muslims in Pakistan. (Don't forget to review the memory verse!)

IV. Optional Cartoon:

Look up Cartoon #42 in the cartoon book and discuss having integrity when taking a test.

Week 12- Making God Famous Through My Attitudes

I. Teaching:

Have you ever really wanted to go somewhere, but in the end you couldn't? How did you feel? How did you respond?

Sometimes we have disappointments in life. We don't always get the things we want, or get to do the things we want to do. When a Cat is disappointed, he throws a fit and gets very upset, often complaining, whining, and blaming God and others. But when a Dog is disappointed, he knows another way to respond.

Dogs know that God is made famous when we maintain a good attitude, so a Dog practices flexibility. Flexibility means we are willing to accept something new and will choose a positive attitude no matter what happens. Although we can't control what happens to us, we can control how we respond. And it pleases God when we choose to respond with a good attitude and show flexibility.

> What if you have been waiting all day to go swimming with your dad after work, but when he comes home he is really tired and wants to take you the next day instead. You feel so disappointed because you really wanted to go!
>
> How would a Cat respond to her dad? How would a Dog respond? Which response would make God famous?
>
> ~~~~~
>
> What if it's your turn to walk your family's new dog, but when it's time to take him on a walk, your mom asks if your brother can walk him instead because he missed his turn yesterday.
>
> How would a Cat respond? How would a Dog? Which response would make God look good?

In either scenario, maybe you could offer a compromise or suggest something that would make you both happy. But the important thing, the thing that makes God famous, is that you try to keep a good attitude no matter what happens, being flexible and open to something new.

II. Memory Verse:

Our memory verse for this week is Philippians 4:4, "Rejoice in the Lord always. I will say it again: Rejoice!"

> **Discuss** what this verse means with your child.

III. Theme Song:

Play Track 1 on the Cat and Dog Audio CD provided in this kit. Have your kids sing along with our curriculum theme song, "We Want To Make God Famous!" See page 196 for the words.

IV. Prayer to Go:

Conclude today's teaching with praying Prayer to Go #20, asking God to be the joy of our life.

"Rejoice in the Lord always." Philippians 4:4

Dear Lord, real joy is found in You not in things, people, or what is happening in my life. Be the joy of my life!

V. The Children's Workbook *(page 67, 68)*:

To finish the day, have your child open to Week 12: Day 1 in The Children's Workbook. Have your student write out the weekly verse and complete the "Word Challenge" activity page. (There is no right or wrong list.)

VI. Optional Activity:

To practice "flexibility," play the Limbo game, or stretch your bodies into the different letters of the alphabet. To make the stretching more of a game, have one person stretch at a time and the others guess which letter is represented.

Making God Famous Through My Attitudes

I. The Children's Workbook (page 69, 70):

> ***Discuss*** the Reflection Question in *The Children's Workbook* for Week 12: Day 2 and have them write down their answer.

Then, look at the Cat and Dog Cartoon and fill in a possible response for the cat and dog. (There is no right or wrong answer.) You'll find the actual cartoon on page 38 in the cartoon book. You may want to look this up to guide your child's possible answer.

> While your child is coloring in the cartoon, ***discuss*** how to respond when we don't get what we want.

II. I Heard Good News Today 2: Big Life:

- Find the country of **Afghanistan** on a globe or the map in *I Heard Good News Today 2: Big Life* on page IX.
- Read Chapter 23, **"A Different Boss,"** in *I Heard Good News Today 2: Big Life* beginning on page 61.

III. The Children's Workbook:

> ***Discuss:*** How did Yusef and his son make God famous in Dilbar's eyes?

Pray for missionaries to be sent to the 8.8 million Tajik Muslims of Afghanistan. (Don't forget to review the memory verse!)

IV. Optional Cartoon:

Look up Cartoon #25 in the cartoon book and discuss how to respond when you've done poorly on a test.

Making God Famous Through My Attitudes

I. The Children's Workbook (page 71, 72):

> **Discuss** the Reflection Question in *The Children's Workbook* for Week 12: Day 3 and have them write down their answer.

Then, look at the Cat and Dog Cartoon and fill in a possible response for the cat and dog. (There is no right or wrong answer.) You'll find the actual cartoon on page 17 in the cartoon book. You may want to look this up to guide your child's possible answer.

> While your child is coloring in the cartoon, **discuss** having a good attitude and thinking of others at the park.

II. *I Heard Good News Today 2: Big Life:*

- Find the country of **Cambodia** on a globe or the map in *I Heard Good News Today 2: Big Life* on page IX.
- Read Chapter 24, **"He Tore Their Family Apart,"** in *I Heard Good News Today 2: Big Life* beginning on page 63.

III. The Children's Workbook:

> **Discuss:** What did God use to make Uong give her life to the Lord?

Pray for missionaries to be sent to the 1.1 million Kinh Buddhists of Cambodia. (Don't forget to review the memory verse!)

IV. Optional Cartoon:

Look up Cartoon #23 in the cartoon book and discuss hitting someone out of anger.

Week 13- Making God Famous
Through My Speech

I. Teaching:

What do you think is the most powerful part of your body?

Did you ever think it might be your tongue? Does your tongue feel very strong? Well it is! Read Proverbs 18:21. It tells us that the tongue has the power of life and death. James tells us our tongues are like a small spark that begins a whole forest fire (James 3:5). Our tongues are very powerful.

And God wants us to use our tongues for good, to glorify Him and make Him famous.

> How do you think you could use your tongue to make God famous?

We can always make God look famous by how we speak to others. We already learned that we should speak honestly, but it makes God famous when we speak kindly as well. In fact, God does not want us to speak anything that is not both kind and honest. And others appreciate that as well!

> *Discuss:* What if you are playing a board game with your family, and you are in the lead. Your sister is losing by a lot and is clearly upset.
>
> What could you say that would be both kind and honest? What could you say that wouldn't be? (Example: bragging vs. encouraging)
>
> ~~~~~
>
> What if you are with some friends, and they begin to tease a boy in the group who wears glasses? They call him "four eyes" and make silly noises.
>
> Are their words both kind and honest? Are they pleasing to God? What could you say that would make God famous?

Although it seems a small part of our body, our tongues are actually a very powerful tool to making someone famous—we need to choose whether that person will be God or ourselves.

II. Memory Verse:

Our memory verse for this week is Ephesians 4:29a, "Do not let any unwhole-some talk come out of your mouths."

> **Discuss** what this verse means with your child.

III. Theme Song:

Play Track 1 on the Cat and Dog Audio CD provided in this kit. Have your kids sing along with our curriculum theme song, "We Want To Make God Famous!" See page 196 for the words.

IV. Prayer to Go:

Conclude today's teaching with praying Prayer to Go #22, asking that our words build others up.

"Do not let any unwholesome talk come out of your mouths, but only what is helpful for building others up according to their needs, so it may benefit those who listen." Ephesians 4:29

Dear Lord, cause me to be very careful about what and how I speak to others. May my words honor Christ and build others up.

V. The Children's Workbook *(page 73, 74)*:

To finish the day, have your child open to Week 13: Day 1 in The Children's Workbook. Have your student write out the weekly verse and complete the "Dialing Dilemma" activity page using a phone key pad. **(Answer: Speak honestly and kindly.)**

VI. Optional Activity:

Cut out a large heart from construction paper. Holding the heart, which you could name to represent a fictional person, say words that are unkind or untruthful and tear the heart a little for each word spoken. Discuss how unkind words hurt deeply and create rips in our heart. Then, speak kind and honest words, and tape up the torn pieces. Does the heart look the same? Our words have lasting effect!

Making God Famous Through My Speech

I. The Children's Workbook *(page 75, 76)*:

> **Discuss** the Reflection Question in *The Children's Workbook* for Week 13: Day 2 and have them write down their answer.

Then, look at the Cat and Dog Cartoon and fill in a possible response for the cat and dog. (There is no right or wrong answer.) You'll find the actual cartoon on page 35 in the cartoon book. You may want to look this up to guide your child's possible answer.

> While your child is coloring in the cartoon, **discuss** whether or not it would please God to join others in singing a song with bad words.

II. I Heard Good News Today 2: Big Life:

- Find the country of **Nepal** on a globe or the map in *I Heard Good News Today 2: Big Life* on page IX.
- Read Chapter 25, **"Their Idols were Powerless,"** in *I Heard Good News Today 2: Big Life* beginning on page 65.

III. The Children's Workbook:

> **Discuss:** What did Asta's sister do to make God famous by her attitudes or actions?

Pray for missionaries to be sent to the 160,000 deaf Nepalese. (Don't forget to review the memory verse!)

IV. Optional Cartoon:

Look up Cartoon #39 in the cartoon book and discuss how lying about being sick does not honor God.

Making God Famous Through My Speech

I. The Children's Workbook (page 77, 78):

> **Discuss** the Reflection Question in *The Children's Workbook* for Week 13: Day 3 and have them write down their answer.

Then, look at the Cat and Dog Cartoon and fill in a possible response for the cat and dog. (There is no right or wrong answer.) You'll find the actual cartoon on page 5 in the cartoon book. You may want to look this up to guide your child's possible answer.

> While your child is coloring in the cartoon, **discuss** responding when you see someone being teased.

II. I Heard Good News Today 2: Big Life:

- Find the country of **Nepal** on a globe or the map in *I Heard Good News Today 2: Big Life* on page IX.
- Read Chapter 26, **"Soul Mate,"** in *I Heard Good News Today 2: Big Life* beginning on page 69.

III. The Children's Workbook:

> **Discuss:** What did Dal's wife and aunt do to make God famous?

Pray for missionaries to be sent to the 67,000 Unreligious Chepang of Nepal. (Don't forget to review the memory verse!)

IV. Optional Cartoon:

Look up Cartoon #40 in *Because He Liked It* and discover a "flying snake!"

Week 14- Making God Famous Through My Compassion

I. Teaching:

Have you ever heard of the word "compassion"?

It's a pretty big word, and it has a pretty important meaning. Compassion means you are concerned about the hurts of others. It means you are willing to "suffer with" them in their pain, whether it's from their hurt body or their hurt heart.

Not only does God tell us to be compassionate towards one another, but over and over again the Bible tells us that God Himself is compassionate! He showed us the way so we can show others. Dogs know that it pleases God when we copy Him by showing compassion to those around us. Cats, however, are only worried about themselves—their own hurts and pains.

> **Discuss:** How do you think a Dog would respond if his brother was sick? How could he show him compassion? How would a Cat respond?
>
> ~~~~~
>
> What if you and your friends were going to play a kickball game, and you knew some of the players were better than others?
> - Would it be compassionate to put all the best players on the same team?
> - Would it be compassionate to make fun of those who missed their kick or couldn't throw the ball very far?
> - Would it be compassionate to encourage everyone who tried to kick?
> - Would it be compassionate to pick some of the younger kids to be on your team first?
>
> ~~~~~
>
> Or what if you are at church with your friends and you notice a new girl standing in the corner? It doesn't seem like she knows anybody, and you know it wouldn't be fun to be standing by yourself. How could you "suffer with" her and show compassion? How would this make God look?

Dogs try to show compassion to everyone around them, whether they are feeling sick or sad. This makes God look good when we are concerned about each other's feelings.

II. Memory Verse:

Our memory verse for this week is Ephesians 4:32, "Be kind and compassionate to one another, forgiving each other, just as in Christ God forgave you."

> ***Discuss*** what this verse means with your child.

III. Theme Song:

Play Track 1 on the Cat and Dog Audio CD provided in this kit. Have your kids sing along with our curriculum theme song, "We Want To Make God Famous!" See page 196 for the words.

IV. Prayer to Go:

Conclude today's teaching with praying Prayer to Go #23, asking God to fill us with His compassion.

"Be kind and compassionate to one another." Ephesians 4:32

Dear Lord, I want to be more like You. Your Word says You are full of compassion, kindness and love. I want these things to be true of me, too.

V. The Children's Workbook *(Page 79, 80)*:

To finish the day, have your child open to Week 14: Day 1 in The Children's Workbook. Have your student write out the weekly verse and complete the "Letter Count" activity page. **(Answer: God is compas-sionate and gracious.)**

VI. Optional Activity:

With your mom, bake some cookies and take them to someone you think may need them or want them! It could be a neighbor, a relative, or maybe a homeless person!

Making God Famous Through My Compassion

I. The Children's Workbook *(page 81, 82)*:

> ***Discuss*** the Reflection Question in *The Children's Workbook* for Week 14: Day 2 and have them write down their answer.

Then, look at the Cat and Dog Cartoon and fill in a possible response for the cat and dog. (There is no right or wrong answer.) You'll find the actual cartoon on page 93 in the cartoon book. You may want to look this up to guide your child's possible answer.

> While your child is coloring in the cartoon, ***discuss*** playing with a child who has special needs.

II. I Heard Good News Today 2: Big Life:

- Find the country of **Nepal** on a globe or the map in *I Heard Good News Today 2: Big Life* on page IX.
- Read Chapter 27, **"Divorce His Wife?,"** in *I Heard Good News Today 2: Big Life* beginning on page 71.

III. The Children's Workbook:

> ***Discuss:*** Name three things God used in Karan's life to make Himself famous in Karan and his wife's eyes.

Pray for missionaries to be sent to the 22,000 Yakha Buddhists of Nepal. (Don't forget to review the memory verse!)

IV. Optional Cartoon:

Look up Cartoon #67 in the cartoon book and discuss being compassionate to a friend when they are scared.

Making God Famous Through My Compassion

I. The Children's Workbook (page 83, 84):

> **Discuss** the Reflection Question in *The Children's Workbook* for Week 14: Day 3 and have them write down their answer.

Then, look at the Cat and Dog Cartoon and fill in a possible response for the cat and dog. (There is no right or wrong answer.) You'll find the actual cartoon on page 98 in the cartoon book. You may want to look this up to guide your child's possible answer.

> While your child is coloring in the cartoon, **discuss** having compassion toward your friends while on the playground.

II. I Heard Good News Today 2: Big Life:

- Find the country of **Afghanistan** on a globe or the map in *I Heard Good News Today 2: Big Life* on page IX.
- Read Chapter 28, **"The Turning Baby,"** in *I Heard Good News Today 2: Big Life* beginning on page 75.

III. The Children's Workbook:

> **Discuss:** Name two things Younis did to make God famous in Farshad's eyes?

Pray for missionaries to be sent to the 11,000 Kowli Gypsy Muslims of Afghanistan. (Don't forget to review the memory verse!)

IV. Optional Cartoon:

Look up Cartoon #92 in the cartoon book and discuss the right and wrong way for children to ask their parents to buy them something in a grocery store.

Week 15- Making God Famous Through My Choices

I. Teaching:

In general, who is a Dog focused on? In general, who is a Cat focused on?

Over the last 14 weeks we have talked about different ways we can make God famous—different ways we can act like a Dog or a Cat. And really, all of them come down to the choices you make.

You choose what words come out of your mouth. You choose your attitude. You choose your behavior.

And it is those choices that can either make God look good to those around you, or make Him unattractive. In fact, the choices you make now not only affect how God looks now, but they will also affect how you make God look in the future. The choices you make now will influence your future.

> Can you think of how a choice you make today will affect the future?
>
> What is a good choice you have made this week, a Dog choice? What is one way you have acted like a Cat this past week?

We will all have moments of acting like both Cats and Dogs, but hopefully, the more we learn about living to make God famous, the more often we will begin to live like a Dog.

We've reached our last day that focuses on making God famous through our own choices. Starting next week, we will begin learning how to make God the most famous He can be! And it's going to take us all around the world.

II. Memory Verse:

Our memory verse for this week is Deuteronomy 30:19b, "Now choose life, so that you and your children may live."

> *Discuss* what this verse means with your child.

III. Theme Song:

Play Track 1 on the Cat and Dog Audio CD provided in this kit. Have your kids sing along with our curriculum theme song, "We Want To Make God Famous!" See page 196 for the words.

IV. Prayer to Go:

Conclude today's teaching with praying Prayer to Go #33, asking God to direct our choices.

> "First seek the counsel of the Lord." 1 Kings 22:5

> *Dear Lord, direct my choices, Lord. Make sure the things I choose to do, no matter how good they seem, are really things You want me to do.*

V. The Children's Workbook *(Page 85, 86)*:

To finish the day, have your child open to Week 15: Day 1 in The Children's Workbook. Have your student write out the weekly verse and complete the "Cross Word Puzzle" activity page. **(Answer: My choices affect God's reputation.)**

VI. Optional Activity:

Let each child take a turn acting out a scenario, and then let the others guess if he/she is exhibiting a Cat or Dog choice. Alternately, the teacher can present a scenario, and then the students have to create either a Cat or Dog response, and the others must guess which one they are representing.

For example: "Two children are going to the playground and see that only one swing is open. They both run to the swing to be the first to jump on, arriving at the same time. They start fighting over who got there first and as a result, who gets to swing first. Are they acting like Cats or Dogs?"

Making God Famous Through My Choices

I. The Children's Workbook *(page 87, 88)*:

> *Discuss* the Reflection Question in *The Children's Workbook* for Week 15: Day 2 and have them write down their answer.

Then, look at the Cat and Dog Cartoon and fill in a possible response for the cat and dog. (There is no right or wrong answer.) You'll find the actual cartoon on page 26 in the cartoon book. You may want to look this up to guide your child's possible answer.

> While your child is coloring in the cartoon, *discuss* choosing to honor God when asked to take out the trash.

II. *I Heard Good News Today 2: Big Life*:

- Find the country of **Cambodia** on a globe or the map in *I Heard Good News Today 2: Big Life* on page IX.
- Read Chapter 29, **"He Kept All The Rituals,"** in *I Heard Good News Today 2: Big Life* beginning on page 79.

III. The Children's Workbook:

> *Discuss:* How did Smoanh make God famous by his attitudes or actions?

Pray for missionaries to be sent to the 225 (not hundred, not thousand, just 225) Unreligious Samre of Cambodia. (Don't forget to review the memory verse!)

IV. Optional Cartoon:

Look up Cartoon #27 in the cartoon book and discuss priorities that honor God. Also talk about the "witness" a Christian has who gets "D's" and "F's" in their grades for class subjects. Is getting really bad grades a good or bad witness?

Making God Famous Through My Choices

I. *The Children's Workbook* (page 89, 90):

> **Discuss** the Reflection Question in *The Children's Workbook* for Week 15: Day 3 and have them write down their answer.

Then, look at the Cat and Dog Cartoon and fill in a possible response for the cat and dog. (There is no right or wrong answer.) You'll find the actual cartoon on page 95 in the cartoon book. You may want to look this up to guide your child's possible answer.

> While your child is coloring in the cartoon, **discuss** how quick obedience makes God famous.

II. *I Heard Good News Today 2: Big Life:*

- Find the country of **India** on a globe or the map in *I Heard Good News Today 2: Big Life* on page IX.
- Read Chapter 30, **"Come,"** in *I Heard Good News Today 2: Big Life* beginning on page 81.

III. *The Children's Workbook:*

> **Discuss:** Write down two things Phillip did to make God famous in Dessaiah's eyes.

Pray for missionaries to be sent to the 1.1 million Wawalud Muslims of India. (Don't forget to review the memory verse!)

IV. *Optional Cartoon:*

Look up Cartoon #24 in *Because He Liked It* and discover birds that surf!

Week 16– The Story of the Bible: Introduction

I. Teaching:

> Guess how many stories there are in the Bible?

Although there are many stories in the Bible, you can also say that the Bible only has **one major** story.

Our Bible was written to be read as one story, with one introduction, one story and one conclusion. And guess who the main character is? It's not us, it's God! And in this story, **God wants to be made famous all over the globe.** And the best way we can make Him famous is by delighting in Him and having a relationship with Him. We were created to make Him famous globally! God wants people from all over the world to have a relationship with Him by delighting in Him and worshiping Him. This is the story that runs from Genesis to Revelation.

Today we're going to talk about the introduction to this story.

Now when God originally created people, "the whole world had one language and a common speech" (Genesis 11:1). But the people's pride was becoming so great that they were only worried about their fame and not God's. So He broke their pride by taking their one language and breaking it down into approximately 70 languages. This happened at the Tower of Babel (Genesis 11:1-9).

> *Discuss:* What would it have been like to be there the day God confused the languages? How would you respond if you were speaking to someone in your language but in the next second, they couldn't understand you and you couldn't understand them! How would you try to find someone whom you could understand?

Those 70 languages split the people into different "people groups," or "ethnic groups." In the Bible, God uses the terms *nations, tribes, tongues,* and *peoples.*

> *Discuss:* What differences can you see between different groups of people today? **(Skin coloring, hair type, dress, height...)**

But because God loves everyone regardless of their language or appearance, He had to have a plan to reach all of them. His plan included all people, but began with one man— Abraham. Next week we'll learn what exactly this plan was.

> *Discuss:* Who has heard of Abraham? What do you know about him already?

II. Memory Verse:

Our memory verse for this week is Psalm 67:1-2, "May God be gracious to us and bless us and make his face shine on us— so that your ways may be known on earth, your salvation among all nations."

III. Theme Song:

Play Track 1 on the Cat and Dog Audio CD provided in this kit. Have your kids sing along with our curriculum theme song, "We Want To Make God Famous!" See page 196 for the words.

IV. Prayer to Go:

Conclude today's teaching with praying Prayer to Go #37 about not being ashamed of the gospel.

"I am not ashamed of the Gospel." Romans 1:16

Dear Lord, I am not ashamed of Your Gospel. Let my life, in what I say and do, show this is true.

V. The Children's Workbook *(Page 91, 92)*:

To finish the day, have your child open to Week 16: Day 1 in the Cat & Dog Children's Workbook. Have your student write out the weekly verse. To see the activity, go to page 182 of *The Children's Workbook* and complete the activity with your child.

VI. Optional Activity:

Sing the chorus of "Our God is an Awesome God," using both the original lyrics and the new lyrics below. Make up hand motions or look up the American Sign Language!

Our God is an awesome God	Our God is a faithful God
He reigns from Heaven above	He keeps His promises
With wisdom, power, and love	To reach all nations
Our God is an awesome God.	Our God is a faithful God.

The Story of the Bible: Introduction

I. The Children's Workbook *(page 93, 94)*:

> ***Discuss*** the Reflection Question in *The Children's Workbook* for Week 16: Day 2 and have them write down their answer.

Look at the cartoon and color in the picture of the Tower of Babel, where God created many different languages.

> While your child is coloring in the cartoon, ***discuss*** the significance of the introduction of the Story of the Bible with your child.

II. I Heard Good News Today 2: Big Life:

- Find the country of **Cambodia** on a globe or the map in *I Heard Good News Today 2: Big Life* on page IX.
- Read Chapter 31, **"Drug Sellers,"** in *I Heard Good News Today 2: Big Life* beginning on page 83.

III. The Children's Workbook:

> ***Discuss:*** Write down two key things God did to make Himself famous in Kou Rath's eyes.

Pray for missionaries to be sent to the 9,000 Unreligious Brao of Cambodia. (Don't forget to review the memory verse!)

IV. Optional Cartoon:

Look up Cartoon #32 in *Because He Liked It!* and discover what's special about the "Aye-Aye" of Madagascar.

The Story of the Bible: Introduction

I. The Children's Workbook *(page 95, 96)*:

> ***Discuss*** the Reflection Question in *The Children's Workbook* for Week 16: Day 3 and have them write down their answer.

Then, look at the Cat and Dog Cartoon and fill in a possible response for the cat and dog. (There is no right or wrong answer.) You'll find the actual cartoon on page 99 in the cartoon book. You may want to use this to guide your child's answer.

> While your child is coloring in the cartoon, ***discuss*** how inviting Christ into your life for the forgiveness of sins is not incorrect, but it is incomplete.

II. I Heard Good News Today 2: Big Life:

- Find the country of **Cambodia** on a globe or the map in *I Heard Good News Today 2: Big Life* on page IX.
- Read Chapter 32, **"It's Too Simple,"** in *I Heard Good News Today 2: Big Life* beginning on page 87.

III. The Children's Workbook:

> ***Discuss:*** What events did God use in Chea's life to make Himself famous to Chea and his wife?

Pray for missionaries to be sent to the 2,300 Unreligious Somray of Cambodia. (Don't forget to review the memory verse!)

IV. Optional Cartoon:

Look up Cartoon #106 in the cartoon book and discuss thinking about others.

Week 17— The Story of the Bible:
Main Theme

I. Teaching:

Do you remember which man we talked about in our last time together, who began God's special plan? (Abraham)

That's right! God chose Abraham to make God famous in all the nations of the earth. His plan unfolds in Genesis, chapter 12. Now to begin his plan, God made a covenant with Abraham. A covenant is a promise that won't be broken.

> What do you think God promised Abraham?

God basically promised Abram two things:

1. God promised **to bless** Abraham greatly with a famous name and to have a big nation come through his family. God also promised to give him protection from his enemies.
2. The other thing God said was that Abraham and his descendants would **be a blessing** to others, making God famous among all the "people groups" of the earth. God wants all nations delighting in Him and worshiping Him.

That blessing to Abraham applies to us today. **Right now, God wants to bless us. And God wants us to be a blessing to the nations.** We are to make God famous to everyone in the whole world. We call these the "Top Line" and the "Bottom Line" of the covenant. If you remember anything about this story, remember this: God wants to bless us greatly (Top Line) and then He wants to use us to bless all the nations (Bottom Line).

It's like God pouring a huge bag of M&M's down from heaven on you and then asking you to eat and enjoy them, but then to turn around and share some of those M&M's with others, both close to you and far away from you.

> **Discuss:** Suppose you were in Sunday school and it was someone's birthday. Their parents brought in enough cupcakes for everyone. But the child didn't want to share them. He only wanted to eat one in class and then eat the rest by himself after church. How would you feel about that?
>
> ~~~~~
>
> How would you feel if God blessed Abraham greatly with a relationship with Him but Abraham never told anyone else about how to have the same relationship with God?

Now how will we know if God kept his promise to Abraham? Well, God has a book in heaven, called *The Register of the Peoples*, in which He is keeping track of every distinct ethnic group that has ever existed on the face of the earth (the Bottom Line). He knows which peoples of the world have been reached with His message and He is constantly updating that book! (Read Psalm 87:4-6.)

Christ's return will not happen until God fulfills His promise to Abraham to redeem people from every tribe, tongue, language, and people. *The Register of the Peoples* is keeping track of that promise.

Today we have talked about the main theme of the Bible: **We are blessed to be a blessing!** Next week, we will peek in the back of the book to see the conclusion to the story!

II. Memory Verse:

Our memory verse for this week is Genesis 12:3: "I will bless those who bless you, and whoever curses you I will curse; and all peoples on earth will be blessed through you."

Discuss what this verse means with your child.

III. Theme Song: (Track 1, *The Children's Workbook*, page 196)

IV. Prayer to Go:

Conclude today's teaching with praying Prayer to Go #38 about having boldness to share Christ with others.

"He who wins souls is wise." Proverbs 11:30

Dear Lord, thank you for the gift of knowing You as my Lord and Saviour. Help me pass this gift on to others. Fill me with God-given boldness to share Christ.

V. The Children's Workbook *(Page 97, 98)*:

To finish the day, have your child open to Week 17: Day 1 in The Children's Workbook. Have your student write out the weekly verse and color "The Story of the Bible" activity page.

VI. Optional Activity:

Create a welcome sign for your home, writing the word "welcome" in a different language! Tape the sign on your front door for one week.

The Story of the Bible: Main Theme

I. The Children's Workbook *(page 99, 100)*:

> ***Discuss*** the Reflection Question in *The Children's Workbook* for Week 17: Day 2 and have them write down their answer. (Please note that the buckets represents "gathering blessings." The Cat wants to keep all of the blessings to themselves, whereas the Dog wants to gather the blessings, enjoy some, and then pass them on to others through the "pipe.")

Then, look at the Cat and Dog Cartoon and fill in a possible response for the cat and dog. (There is no right or wrong answer.) You'll find the actual cartoon on page 50 in the cartoon book. You may want to use this to guide your child's answer.

> While your child is coloring in the cartoon, ***discuss*** different attitudes at Christmastime. Which best reflects the Abrahamic Covenant?

II. *I Heard Good News Today 2: Big Life:*

- Find the country of ***India*** on a globe or the map in *I Heard Good News Today 2: Big Life* on page IX.
- Read Chapter 33, **"He Never Lost Hope,"** in *I Heard Good News Today 2: Big Life* beginning on page 89.

III. The Children's Workbook:

> ***Discuss:*** How did Namanthya make God look bad and how did he make God look famous?

Pray for missionaries to be sent to the 7.3 million Santal Hindus of India. (Don't forget to review the memory verse!)

IV. Optional Cartoon:

Look up Cartoon #71 in the cartoon book and discuss different attitudes at birthday parties.

The Story of the Bible: Main Theme

I. The Children's Workbook (page 101, 102):

> **Discuss** the Reflection Question in *The Children's Workbook* for Week 17: Day 3 and have them write down their answer.

Then, look at the Cat and Dog Cartoon and fill in a possible response for the cat and dog. (There is no right or wrong answer.) You'll find the actual cartoon on page 32 in the cartoon book. You may want to use this to guide your child's answer.

> While your child is coloring in the cartoon, **discuss** sharing with others.

II. I Heard Good News Today 2: Big Life:

- Find the country of **Afghanistan** on a globe or the map in *I Heard Good News Today 2: Big Life* on page IX.
- Read Chapter 34, **"A Martyr?,"** in *I Heard Good News Today 2: Big Life* beginning on page 91.

III. The Children's Workbook:

> **Discuss** What did God use in Shabbir's life to bring Shabbir to Himself? And how did Shabbir make God famous by his attitudes or actions?

Pray for missionaries to be sent to the 2,200 Parya Muslims of Afghanistan. (Don't forget to review the memory verse!)

IV. Optional Cartoon:

Look up Cartoon #84 in the cartoon book and discuss fighting over who goes first.

Week 18- The Story of the Bible:
Conclusion

I. Teaching:

> **Discuss:** Who remembers the main theme of the Story of the Bible?
> **(We are blessed to be a blessing!)**

Yes, like Abraham, we have been blessed by God to bless all nations. Now before we peek into the back of the book to find the conclusion, we should ask, how do we know this is really important? Did Jesus say anything about the Top Line and Bottom Line of the covenant?

Can you think of any time Jesus talked about this covenant?

In Luke 24:45-47, Jesus is in the very last days of His life. With His disciples, He summarizes God's Word (only the Old Testament at that time) into two simple parts: "*The Christ will suffer and rise from the dead on the third day,* and *repentance and forgiveness of sins will be preached in his name to all nations, beginning at Jerusalem.*" The blessing of eternal life because of Christ's resurrection is our top-line blessing, and the responsibility to tell all nations about Him is our bottom-line responsibility!

Because Jesus only had the Old Testament to read, this means The Great Commission of reaching all nations began in Genesis!

> **Discuss:** Since Abraham lived 2,000 years before Christ, how old was the Great Commission when Jesus walked on the earth? (2,000 years old.) How old is the Great Commission today? **(4,000 years old.)**
> ~~~~
> Did Jesus want his disciples to just tell the people in Jerusalem about Him? Just in their state? Just in their country? Where? **(Everywhere! The whole world!)**

Look up and read Matthew 28:18-20. The main verb in this passage is "make disciples." It tells us we are to disciple all nations. This means making God famous to every people group! This action is accomplished by baptizing people and teaching them to obey Jesus' commands. What results when you have people identifying with Christ and following his commands? A new church! So Jesus was trying to communicate for us *to go and start a church for every ethnic group on earth.*

> Was this commandment new to the disciples? **(No.)** Where do we first see it in the Bible? **(Genesis 12:1-3)**

So we now know that the two parts of the covenant to Abraham were confirmed by Jesus and are actually given as commands for us to obey. We've heard the introduction and the main theme of the story, so what about the ending? Does God keep His promise to Abraham?

It's time to peek in the back of the book: open and read Revelation 5:9-10. Here, in this future picture, we see the Lamb of God (Jesus) being worshiped because He has saved people from every tongue, tribe, and nation! Amen!

> When we get to Heaven, who will we see there? **(Relatives, Bible heroes, believers who have already died who know the Lord...)** Who else? **(People who love God from all around the world!)**

So in the end, God will complete what He planned to do.

II. Memory Verse:

Our memory verse for this week is Psalm 67:7, "God will bless us, and all the ends of the earth will fear him."

> *Discuss* what this verse means with your child.

III. Theme Song: (Track 1, *The Children's Workbook*, page 196)

IV. Prayer to Go: (#39)

"Sing to the Lord, praise His name, proclaim His salvation day after day."
Psalm 96

Dear Lord, I ask that You would use my life to point others to Jesus Christ.

V. The Children's Workbook *(Page 103, 104):*

To finish the day, have your child open to Week 18: Day 1 in The Children's Workbook. Have your student write out the weekly verse and color the "Revelation 5:9-10" activity page.

VI. Optional Activity:

Around the World Game! Have each player take turns naming a country starting with the letters of the alphabet—A to Z. They can use a map to help, but no country names can be repeated. Winner is the first to complete the alphabet, or whoever has named the most countries in a preset length of time. (Taken from *Great Global Activities* by Bev Gundersen.)

The Story of the Bible: The Conclusion

I. The Children's Workbook (page 105, 106):

> Discuss the Reflection Question in The Children's Workbook for Week 18: Day 2 and have them write down their answer.

Look at the cartoon and color in the picture of the "Register of the Peoples." Talk about the significance of there being people from every tongue, tribe, and nation in Heaven.

> While your child is coloring in the cartoon, discuss the significance of there being people from every tongue, tribe, and nation in Heaven.

II. I Heard Good News Today 2: Big Life:

- Find the country of India on a globe or the map in I Heard Good News Today 2: Big Life on page IX.
- Read Chapter 35, "An Angry Mob," in I Heard Good News Today 2: Big Life beginning on page 95.

III. The Children's Workbook:

> Discuss: What price did Jadab have to pay to make God famous?

Pray for missionaries to be sent to the 1.1 million Mudiraj Hindus of India. (Don't forget to review the memory verse!)

IV. Optional Cartoon:

Look up Cartoon #80 in the cartoon book and discuss having a good attitude when you can't do everything you'd like.

The Story of the Bible: The Conclusion

I. *The Children's Workbook* (page 107, 108):

> ***Discuss*** the Reflection Question in *The Children's Workbook* for Week 18: Day 3 and have them write down their answer.

Then, look at the Cat and Dog Cartoon and fill in a possible response for the cat and dog. (There is no right or wrong answer.) You'll find the actual cartoon on page 43 in the cartoon book. You may want to use this to guide your child's answer.

> While your child is coloring in the cartoon, ***discuss*** what it means to pray for the entire world—not just our little world.

II. *I Heard Good News Today 2: Big Life:*

- Find the country of **Nepal** on a globe or the map in *I Heard Good News Today 2: Big Life* on page IX.
- Read Chapter 36, **"The Perfect, Empty Life,"** in *I Heard Good News Today 2: Big Life* beginning on page 97.

III. *The Children's Workbook:*

> ***Discuss*** What did Sunita do to make God famous in her husband's eyes?

Pray for missionaries to be sent to the 1.3 million Magar Hindus of Nepal. (Don't forget to review the memory verse!)

IV. *Optional Cartoon:*

Look up Cartoon #48 in *Because He Liked It!* and discover a super frog!

Week 19– Blessed to be a Blessing

I. Teaching: (*You will need a bag of M&Ms for this day*)

> **Review:** How many parts were in the promise God gave to Abraham? **(2)** What were the two parts? **(Top Line, Bottom Line)**

Did you know that we, as followers of Christ, are called children of Abraham? It's true! (Read Galatians 3:7.) So the promise and blessing given to Abraham now applies to us. So what does it mean to us to be blessed by God?

> **Discuss:** Engage the children in a discussion of what it means to be blessed by God. How are they blessed right here where they live (i.e. food, clothing, houses, education, parents, etc.)? Follow that discussion with questions such as: Do all the children in the world have enough food to eat? Do all children have a house to live in? Do all children know where their parents are?

Following that discussion, if you have more than one child participating, divide the group in half. Have one group stand and hold their hands cupped together. Have them remain standing as you pour M&Ms (or something similar) into their hands as they tell you one of the blessings they are thankful for. When you have finished, ask the question:

- If God has given you a special blessing and not the other children, does that mean He loves you more? (The answer is "no," God loves everyone the same.)
- Well, what does God want you to do with that special blessing? (Share it!) Then have those who have received the special blessing of M&Ms share half their M&Ms with someone who did not receive that blessing. This is a concrete way of communicating the need to pass the blessing on to others. (They've been blessed to be a blessing.)

> **Discuss:** Now to whom are we to pass the blessing? **(Our family and friends, yes, but also all the nations of the world.)**

Around the world, about 1 out of every 4 people has never heard of Jesus and has no one to tell them. How can God be famous in their eyes if they've never heard of Him? Even these unreached peoples are included in the blessing!

> **Review** the introduction, main theme, and conclusion of the Story of the Bible.

II. Memory Verse:

Our memory verse for this week is Psalm 96:3, "Declare his glory among the nations, his marvelous deeds among all peoples."

Discuss what this verse means with your child.

III. Theme Song: (Track 1, *The Children's Workbook*, page 196)

IV. Prayer to Go:

Conclude today's teaching with praying Prayer to Go #40 about impacting the world for Christ.

> "Declare his glory among the nations, his marvelous deeds among all peoples." Psalm 96:3

> *Dear Lord, I pray that people from all nations will come to know, love and worship You. Make me aware of how I can impact the world for Your glory today.*

V. The Children's Workbook (Page 109, 110):

To finish the day, have your child open to Week 19: Day 1 in The Children's Workbook. Have your student write out the weekly verse and color the "Blessed To Be A Blessing" activity page.

VI. Optional Activity:

Using a familiar song, create new lyrics that reflect the Story of the Bible. (For example, use Old McDonald, Twinkle Twinkle, Jesus Loves Me, Away in a Manger...)

An example is given below:

"The B-I-B-L-E"

> **The B-I-B-L-E**
> **It has one story you see,**
> **To reach all nations with God's love,**
> **The B-I-B-L-E**
> **Missions!**

Blessed to be a Blessing!

I. *The Children's Workbook* (page 111, 112):

> ***Discuss*** the Reflection Question in *The Children's Workbook* for Week 19: Day 2 and have them write down their answer.

Then, look at the Cat and Dog Cartoon. This was taken out of our original cartoon book of *101 Differences Between Cats and Dogs*.

> While your child is looking at the cartoon, ***discuss*** different ways to handle God's blessings.

II. *I Heard Good News Today 2: Big Life:*

- Find the country of **Nepal** on a globe or the map in *I Heard Good News Today 2: Big Life* on page IX.
- Read Chapter 37, **"Two Charging Boars,"** in *I Heard Good News Today 2: Big Life* beginning on page 99.

III. *The Children's Workbook:*

> ***Discuss*** three things God did in Kirrin's life to make Himself famous and have your child list them.

Pray for missionaries to be sent to the 123,000 Unreligious Sunwar of Nepal. (Don't forget to review the memory verse!)

IV. *Optional Cartoon:*

Look up Cartoon #45 in the cartoon book and discuss ways to glorify God at a group dinner.

Blessed to be a Blessing!

I. *The Children's Workbook* (page 113, 114):

> ***Discuss*** the Reflection Question in *The Children's Workbook* for Week 19: Day 3 and have them write down their answer.

Color the cartoon of kids from different countries.

> While your child is coloring in the cartoon, ***discuss*** how different isn't wrong, it's just different and reflects God's glory in greater ways!

II. *I Heard Good News Today 2: Big Life:*

- Find the country of ***Cambodia*** on a globe or the map in *I Heard Good News Today 2: Big Life* on page IX.
- Read Chapter 38, **"A Paralyzed Mother,"** in *I Heard Good News Today 2: Big Life* beginning on page 103.

III. *The Children's Workbook:*

> ***Discuss*** What made God famous in Uma's eyes and how long did it take?

Pray for missionaries to be sent to the 30,000 Unreligious Phnong of Cambodia. (Don't forget to review the memory verse!)

IV. *Optional Cartoon:*

Look up Cartoon #46 in the cartoon book and discuss what to do if you're given too much change.

Week 20- David and Goliath

I. Teaching:

> **Discuss** what you know about the story of David and Goliath.

Did you know that the story of David and Goliath also has a Top Line and Bottom Line?

Read 1 Samuel 17:45-47. If you'd like, act out the entirety of the story.

> **Discuss:** What do you think the Top Line blessing is?

The Top Line message of the story is found in verse 45: God can help us defeat our enemies (even giants) with even the small abilities we bring to Him as we put our trust in His name. David had only stones and a sling, but the battle belonged to God, and so God brought the victory for David.

> **Discuss:** Where do you see a Bottom Line responsibility? Why did David fight Goliath?

In verse 46, David said he fought Goliath so that **the whole world would know that there is a God in Israel.** David was making God famous globally! God blessed David with victory, and He wanted David to tell the world about Him.

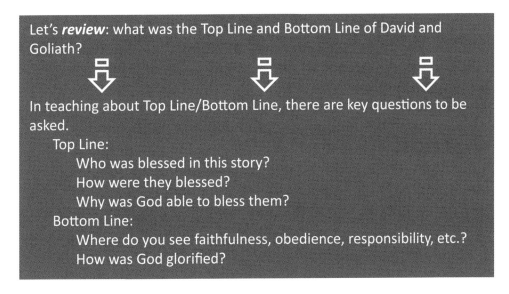

Let's **review**: what was the Top Line and Bottom Line of David and Goliath?

In teaching about Top Line/Bottom Line, there are key questions to be asked.
   Top Line:
      Who was blessed in this story?
      How were they blessed?
      Why was God able to bless them?
   Bottom Line:
      Where do you see faithfulness, obedience, responsibility, etc.?
      How was God glorified?

II. Memory Verse:

Our memory verse for this week is Habakkuk 2:14, "For the earth will be filled with the knowledge of the glory of the LORD as the waters cover the sea."

> ***Discuss*** what this verse means with your child emphasizing "as the waters cover the sea."

III. Theme Song: (Track 1, *The Children's Workbook*, page 196)

IV. Prayer to Go:

Conclude today's teaching with praying Prayer to Go #41, that all we do will bring glory to God.

"Let your light shine before men that they may see your good works and glorify your Father in heaven." Matthew 5:16

Dear Lord, let all that I do bring glory to Your name.

V. The Children's Workbook *(Page 115, 116):*

To finish the day, have your child open to Week 20: Day 1 in The Children's Workbook. Have your student write out the weekly verse and complete the "David and Goliath" activity page.

VI. Optional Activity:

Many cultures can't read or write. As a result, storytelling is an important part of that culture. Often, the storyteller is the most revered teacher. Have the children imagine they were working with a tribe that has no Bible or written language, so they must be the storytellers of God's truth. Read the story of David and Goliath again and have the children try to retell it themselves, as if someone was hearing it for the first time. Check:
- Did they get all the important details?
- How could they use their voices to keep the story interesting?
- Are they looking the listener in the eye?
- Could any body gestures help?

(Taken from Bev Gunderson, *Great Global Activities*.)

DaVid aňd G̤oliaᵗh

I. The Children's Workbook (page 117, 118):

> **Discuss** the Reflection Question in *The Children's Workbook* for Week 20: Day 2 and have them write down their answer.

Then, look at the Cat and Dog Cartoon and fill in a possible response for the cat and dog. (There is no right or wrong answer.) You'll find the actual cartoon on page 63 in the cartoon book. You may want to use this to guide your child's answer.

> While your child is coloring in the cartoon, **discuss** different perspectives on visiting a grandparent in the hospital. What is the grandparent's perspective? What about the parent's perspective? What about the child's perspective? What is God's perspective?

II. I Heard Good News Today 2: Big Life:

- Find the country of **India** on a globe or the map in *I Heard Good News Today 2: Big Life* on page IX.
- Read Chapter 39, **"Thanking God for Evil Spirits,"** in *I Heard Good News Today 2: Big Life* beginning on page 105.

III. The Children's Workbook:

> **Discuss:** What power did God display to make Himself famous in Mairum's eyes?

Pray for missionaries to be sent to the 35,000 Unreligious Yimchungra of India. (Don't forget to review the memory verse!)

IV. Optional Cartoon:

Look up Cartoon #96 in the cartoon book and discuss respecting safety rules.

David and Goliath

I. The Children's Workbook *(page 119, 120)*:

> ***Discuss*** the Reflection Question in *The Children's Workbook* for Week 20: Day 3 and have them write down their answer.

Then, look at the Cat and Dog Cartoon and fill in a possible response for the cat and dog. (There is no right or wrong answer.) You'll find the actual cartoon on page 86 in the cartoon book. You may want to use this to guide your child's answer.

> While your child is coloring in the cartoon, ***discuss*** having a good attitude when you lose.

II. *I Heard Good News Today 2: Big Life:*

- Find the country of **Nepal** on a globe or the map in *I Heard Good News Today 2: Big Life* on page IX.
- Read Chapter 40, **"Standing Tall for Jesus,"** in *I Heard Good News Today 2: Big Life* beginning on page 107.

III. *The Children's Workbook:*

> ***Discuss:*** List two powerful things the Christians did in Lal's life to make God famous.

Pray for missionaries to be sent to 173,000 Unreligious Western-Gurung of Nepal. (Don't forget to review the memory verse!)

IV. *Optional Cartoon:*

Go to Cartoon #86 in *Because He Liked It!* and discover how much the Blue Whale's tongue weighs!

Week 21- Daniel & the Lion's Den

I. Teaching:

What is your favorite animal at the zoo? Would you like to spend the night with that animal in your house? What if it was a lion?

Read Daniel 6:16-27. Act out the story.

> *Discuss:* What do you think the Top Line blessing is in this story?

In verses 19-23, we see that God rescued Daniel from harm, and we learn that God will rescue us when we are in trouble if we are seeking Him and trusting Him.

> *Discuss:* What about the Bottom Line? What is the Bottom Line message from this story?

Once Daniel was rescued from the den, the *Gentile king wrote to all peoples that in every part of his kingdom people must fear and reverence the God of Daniel because He is the living God.* Wow! A Gentle king sends out a decree to all the world that everyone must worship God? He was making God famous! God was glorified and revealed to all peoples of the earth.

> *Review:* What was the Top Line and Bottom Line of Daniel and the Lion's Den?

II. Memory Verse:

Our memory verse for this week is Psalm 47:2, "How awesome is the Lord Most High, the great King over all the earth!"

> *Discuss* what this verse means with your child.

III. Theme Song: (Track 1, *The Children's Workbook*, page 196)

IV. Prayer to Go:

Conclude today's teaching with praying Prayer to Go #42, asking that our example would point others to Christ.

"Follow my example, as I follow the example of Christ." 1 Corinthians 11:1

Dear Lord, I want to make Your name known so others will know, love and worship You by my example. Cause me to be very careful about the way I behave so that my life points others to You.

V. The Children's Workbook *(Page 121, 122)*:

To finish the day, have your child open to Week 21: Day 1 in The Children's Workbook. Have your student write out the weekly verse and complete the "Daniel and the Lion's Den" activity page. There is one word per line. The words are: *The king texted all the other kings, "Worship the God of Daniel."* Here is a Gentile king evangelizing a Gentile world—the Bottom Line.

VI. Optional Activity:

Another week of storytelling! Once again, have the children imagine they were working with a tribe that has no Bible or written language, so they must be the storytellers of God's truth. Read the story of Daniel and the Lion's Den again and have the children try to retell it themselves, as if someone was hearing it for the first time. Check:
- Did they get all the important details?
- How could they use their voices to keep the story interesting?
- Are they looking the listener in the eye?
- Could any body gestures help?

(Taken from Bev Gunderson, *Great Global Activities*.)

Daniel and the Lion's Den

I. The Children's Workbook (page 123, 124):

> **Discuss** the Reflection Question in *The Children's Workbook* for Week 21: Day 2 and have them write down their answer.

Then, look at the Cat and Dog Cartoon and fill in a possible response for the cat and dog. (There is no right or wrong answer.) You'll find the actual cartoon on page 51 in the cartoon book. You may want to use this to guide your child's answer.

> While your child is coloring in the cartoon, **discuss** thinking of your family above yourself.

II. I Heard Good News Today 2: Big Life:

- Find the country of **Nepal** on a globe or the map in *I Heard Good News Today 2: Big Life* on page IX.
- Read Chapter 41, **"A Proud Heart,"** in *I Heard Good News Today 2: Big Life* beginning on page 111.

III. The Children's Workbook:

> **Discuss:** What did God have to break in Buddhi to make Himself famous to him?

Pray for missionaries to be sent to the 7,300 Lhomi Buddhists of Nepal. (Don't forget to review the memory verse!)

IV. Optional Cartoon:

Look up Cartoon #56 in the cartoon book and discuss having integrity.

Daniel and the Lion's Den

I. The Children's Workbook (page 125, 126):

> *Discuss* the Reflection Question in *The Children's Workbook* for Week 21: Day 3 and have them write down their answer.

Then, look at the Cat and Dog Cartoon and fill in a possible response for the cat and dog. (There is no right or wrong answer.) You'll find the actual cartoon on page 6 in the cartoon book. You may want to use this to guide your child's answer.

> While your child is coloring in the cartoon, *discuss* ways you can show love to your dad. Also talk about how it makes dad feel!

II. I Heard Good News Today 2: Big Life:

- Find the country of **Nepal** on a globe or the map in *I Heard Good News Today 2: Big Life* on page IX.
- Read Chapter 42, **"Millions of Gods,"** in *I Heard Good News Today 2: Big Life* beginning on page 113.

III. The Children's Workbook:

> *Discuss:* How did the Christian make God famous by his attitudes or actions and how did Lolita's village respond?

Pray for missionaries to be sent to the 1.6 million Newar Hindus of Nepal. (Don't forget to review the memory verse!)

IV. Optional Cartoon:

Look up Cartoon #58 in *Because He Liked It!* and learn why the spider can go a year without eating!

Week 22- Feeding the 5,000 & 4,000

I. Teaching:

Have you ever been really hungry? What if you were really hungry and there was nowhere close to get food?

Today, we're going to look at two similar but different stories from the New Testament. Read Matthew 14:13-21 and Matthew 15:29-39.

> Imagine what it would have been like to be there that day: How would you feel after spending a day with your parents listening to Jesus? What would you think when Jesus started passing around the 5 loaves and 2 fish as if it were going to feed all these people? How much did you eat when it came to you? How would you have felt after seeing the miracle performed?

Why is the story in the Bible twice? In the first story, where there were 12 baskets left over, Jesus was feeding 5,000 Jewish men. In the second story, Jesus was teaching Gentiles, so the 4,000 fed were Gentiles. (This is why the disciples didn't have faith that He could feed the 4,000 even though He'd already fed 5,000.)

> **Discuss** what is the Top Line to these stories?
> **(Answer: In the feeding of the 5,000, Jesus cared enough to meet the physical needs of His own people, the Jews.)**

Just about everywhere you find a Top Line, you'll find a Bottom Line.

> And what is the Bottom Line message?
> **(Answer: In the feeding of the 4,000, Jesus wanted to show He also had compassion for the Gentiles [non-Jewish people] on the other side of the Sea of Galilee!)**

Again, Jesus is showing us that He is concerned with blessing both Abraham's descents, the Jews (the Top Line), as well as all the nations on earth (the Bottom Line). For us today, that means that Jesus not only loves every American, but He loves every Muslim, Buddhist, Hindu—everyone on the face of the earth!

II. Memory Verse:

Our memory verse for this week is Psalm 46:10, "Be still and know that I am God; I will be exalted among the nations, I will be exalted in the earth."

III. *Theme Song:* (Track 1, *The Children's Workbook*, page 196)

IV. *Prayer to Go:*

Conclude today's teaching with praying Prayer to Go #43, asking God to keep us from doing anything that would keep others from Him.

"Be very careful, then, how you live—not as unwise but as wise." Ephesians 5:15

Dear Lord, keep me from doing anything that would turn others away from You.

V. *The Children's Workbook (Page 127, 128):*

To finish the day, have your child open to Week 22: Day 1 in The Children's Workbook. Have your student write out the weekly verse and complete "The Alphabetical Country Challenge!" activity page. (When you get stuck, simply Google "List all nations alphabetically;" this will bring up a list quite quickly! All but the letter "X" have one.)

VI. *Optional Activity:*

Create a Children Around the World Chain! Fold a piece of paper into fourths, accordion style. Trace the pattern of a child on one of the outside sections. Be sure the hands and feet are on the folds. Cut the child pattern out, leaving the hands and feet uncut. Then open the folds and decorate the paper children as desired, looking up clothing around the world to accurately dress the dolls! If you make multiple chains, you can combine them for a border or door decoration.

(Taken from Bev Gundersen's, *Animist Factivities*.)

Feeding of the 5,000 & 4,000

I. *The Children's Workbook* (page 129, 130):

> ***Discuss*** the Reflection Question in *The Children's Workbook* for Week 22: Day 2 and have them write down their answer.

Then, look at the Cat and Dog Cartoon and fill in a possible response for the cat and dog. (There is no right or wrong answer.) You'll find the actual cartoon on page 70 in the cartoon book. You may want to use this to guide your child's answer.

> While your child is coloring in the cartoon, ***discuss*** how showing kindness to your neighbors can make God famous.

II. *I Heard Good News Today 2: Big Life:*

- Find the country of ***Afghanistan*** on a globe or the map in *I Heard Good News Today 2: Big Life* on page IX.
- Read Chapter 43, **"The Mysterious Book,"** in *I Heard Good News Today 2: Big Life* beginning on page 115.

III. *The Children's Workbook:*

> ***Discuss:*** What did God do to make Himself famous in the eyes of both shepherds?

Pray for missionaries to be sent to the 9,700 Kho Muslims of Afghanistan. (Don't forget to review the memory verse!)

IV. *Optional Cartoon:*

Look up Cartoon #61 in the cartoon book and discuss praying before a meal.

Feeding of the 5,000 & 4,000

I. The Children's Workbook *(page 131, 132)*:

> ***Discuss*** the Reflection Question in *The Children's Workbook* for Week 22: Day 3 and have them write down their answer.

Then, look at the Cat and Dog Cartoon and fill in a possible response for the cat and dog. (There is no right or wrong answer.) You'll find the actual cartoon on page 81 in the cartoon book. You may want to use this to guide your child's answer.

> While your child is coloring in the cartoon, ***discuss*** whether making fun of someone with braces makes God famous or not.

II. *I Heard Good News Today 2: Big Life:*

- Find the country of ***India*** on a globe or the map in *I Heard Good News Today 2: Big Life* on page IX.
- Read Chapter 44, **"The Search for Truth,"** in *I Heard Good News Today 2: Big Life* beginning on page 119.

III. *The Children's Workbook:*

> ***Discuss:*** What was Butta searching for that led him to see God as famous and what did God use to finally show him?

Pray for missionaries to be sent to the 1.6 million Nai Hindus of India. (Don't forget to review the memory verse!)

IV. *Optional Cartoon:*

Look up Cartoon #87 in the cartoon book and discuss balancing schoolwork and play.

Week 23- Paul Teaching the Gentiles

I. Teaching:

When God spoke to Abraham to be a blessing to the nations, he was only one man. But God said, "I'll use you and your children to bless the nations."

After Jesus walked on the earth, He wanted to keep getting the word out that God's Son had come to earth to save all of the peoples of the earth. In Acts 1:8, He told His disciples to tell the good news in Jerusalem, *and* Judea, *and* Samaria *and* to the ends of the earth! But unfortunately, in Acts 1-7, they stayed in Jerusalem and never got out. But God sent them out through persecution. (Acts 8:1)

Once the persecution started, He again chose one of Abraham's descendants to tell others. His name was Saul. He started out an enemy of Jesus by persecuting the church, but later became a follower. His named was changed to Paul. We now call him the Apostle Paul.

> Have you heard of the Apostle Paul? What do you know about him?

God used Paul mightily to fulfill the Bottom Line of his covenant because the disciples only thought that God's love was for the Jews. In the beginning, they didn't think the Gentiles were loved by God nor did they think Gentiles could love God.

Read and summarize Acts 26:12-23 and Romans 15:14-21.

As we look at Paul's life and how God dramatically changed him, we see God giving him the blessing of salvation, not because he deserved it or even desired it, but because God chose him. God gave Paul a vision for the world around him and Paul was obedient to reach out to the people who weren't Jews, the Gentiles.

> *Discuss:* What is the Top Line of Paul's life and ministry? How did God bless Paul? Why did God choose Paul? How was God glorified through Paul's ministry?
> **(Answer: Paul received personal salvation, God helped and protected Paul as he preached to the Gentiles, to take the Good News to the Gentiles, and God gave power to Paul to do miracles.)**

Remember, just about everywhere you see a Top Line, you'll find a Bottom Line.

> *Discuss:* What was the Bottom Line?
> **(Answer: Paul was sent to preach the Good News of Jesus to not only his own people but to the Gentiles all around him, to those who had never been told about Jesus.)**

II. Memory Verse:

Our memory verse for this week is Matthew 24:14, "And this gospel of the kingdom will be preached in the whole world as a testimony to all nations, and then the end will come."

> **Discuss** what this verse means with your child.

III. Theme Song: (Track 1, *The Children's Workbook*, page 196)

IV. Prayer to Go: (#44)

"No one can come to me unless the Father who sent me draws him." John 6:44

Dear Lord, I have family and friends who do not have a relationship with You. They cannot bring You glory because they do not know You. Please draw them to You so that they will know, love and worship You.

V. The Children's Workbook *(Page 133, 134)*:

To finish the day, have your child open to Week 23: Day 1 in The Children's Workbook. Have your student write out the weekly verse and complete "The Gentile Challenge" activity page showing which children are Gentiles. (The boy in the top right is the only Jew.)

VI. Optional Activity:

Divide into two groups. Pretend you are interacting with a people group across the world and you must learn their customs. Have each team secretly make up 1-3 rules that their people group applies to a certain area of culture, like greetings, food, or dress. Then, come together and interact, trying to discover the others' rules.

Example rules for eating: (Taken from *Great Global Games* by Bev Gundersen.)

Team 1
1. You can only hold utensils with your right hand.
2. Food is always passed to the right.
3. The person on the left dishes up for him.

Team 2
1. You can't use utensils.
2. Everyone eats out of a common bowl.
3. People help themselves.

Paul Teaching the Gentiles

I. The Children's Workbook *(page 135, 136)*:

> ***Discuss*** the Reflection Question in *The Children's Workbook* for Week 23: Day 2 and have them write down their answer.

Then, look at the Cat and Dog Cartoon and fill in a possible response for the cat and dog. (There is no right or wrong answer.) You'll find the actual cartoon on page 60 in the cartoon book. You may want to use this to guide your child's answer.

> While your child is coloring in the cartoon, ***discuss*** what they can do when they see someone different in a group they are in.

II. I Heard Good News Today 2: Big Life:

- Find the country of ***Afghanistan*** on a globe or the map in *I Heard Good News Today 2: Big Life* on page IX.
- Read Chapter 45, **"A Small Scrap of Paper,"** in *I Heard Good News Today 2: Big Life* beginning on page 121.

III. The Children's Workbook:

> ***Discuss*** How did God make Himself famous in the eyes of Faizal?

Pray for missionaries to be sent to the 119,000 deaf Muslims in Afghanistan. (Don't forget to review the memory verse!)

IV. Optional Cartoon:

Look up Cartoon #68 in the cartoon book and discuss different responses to preparing for another year of school.

Paul Teaching the Gentiles

I. *The Children's Workbook* (page 137, 138):

> ***Discuss*** the Reflection Question in *The Children's Workbook* for Week 23: Day 3 and have them write down their answer.

Then, look at the Cat and Dog Cartoon and fill in a possible response for the cat and dog. (There is no right or wrong answer.) You'll find the actual cartoon on page 83 in the cartoon book. You may want to use this to guide your child's answer.

> While your child is coloring in the cartoon, ***discuss*** having your grandparent come and live with you.

II. *I Heard Good News Today 2: Big Life:*

- Find the country of **Nepal** on a globe or the map in *I Heard Good News Today 2: Big Life* on page IX.
- Read Chapter 46, **"The Unexpected Tiger,"** in *I Heard Good News Today 2: Big Life* beginning on page 123.

III. *The Children's Workbook:*

> ***Discuss:*** What did Phillip do right before God made Himself famous to the Christians?

Pray for missionaries to be sent to 3,400 Unreligious Koi of Nepal. (Don't forget to review the memory verse!)

IV. *Optional Cartoon:*

Look up Cartoon #13 in the cartoon book and discuss whether a clean yard or messy yard makes God look good.

Week 24- T is for Tribals

I. Teaching:

There are lots of religions that don't know about God's love for us through Jesus. There are the Muslims, the Buddhists, the Hindus, the Tribal peoples—and a large number of people that are simply unreligious. They don't even believe God exists at all. How can we remember them all?

Can you show me your thumb? What do you use your thumb to do?

Today we are going to use our thumbs to learn about people God loves who have never heard of Jesus! Now that we know it has always been God's heart to reach all peoples, we want to learn more about the people who are still unreached.

To help us remember the unreached peoples, we will use the acronym T.H.U.M.B. T stands for Tribal, H for Hindu, U for Unreligious, M for Muslim and B for Buddhist.

> **Discuss:** What is the first letter in the word thumb? And what does T stand for? **(Tribal!)**

Today we will learn about tribal peoples. They live mainly in Africa and Southeast Asia. Look on the world map on page 181 in *The Children's Workbook* and see if you can identify where they live.

Tribals generally live in small villages and believe differently depending on their location. Fear controls tribal peoples' lives. They believe everything has a spirit, even trees and rocks and the sun. They believe they have to keep in right relationship with all these spirits or else those spirits may harm them.

> **Action Step:** Go outside and look at a tree or rock. Try to imagine a spirit living inside it and try to imagine what you should do to make it happy.

Tribals also believe in witch doctors or holy men that can heal using lotions, potions, magic stones, and evil and good spirits. Worshiping many different spirits is done individually or by families. Many times they believe that when you die, you come back as a spirit.

> **Discuss:** How do you think tribal people view Jesus? As Christians, does God want us to live in fear like the tribal people?

II. Memory Verse:

Our memory verse for this week is Matthew 28:19, "Therefore, go, and make disciples of all nations, baptizing them in the name of the Father and of the Son and of the Holy Spirit."

> **Discuss** what this verse means with your child.

III. Theme Song: (Track 1, *The Children's Workbook*, page 196)

IV. Prayer to Go:

Conclude today's teaching with praying Prayer to Go #45, asking God to send workers into His harvest fields.

"The harvest is plentiful but the workers are few." Matthew 9:37

Dear Lord, so many people in this world have never heard Your name or given You praise. Lord, I am willing to be used as a worker in Your harvest fields.

V. The Children's Workbook *(Page 139, 140)*:

To finish the day, have your child open to Week 24: Day 1 in The Children's Workbook. Have your student write out the weekly verse and read the story about Ekeria, the little Tribal girl.

VI. Optional Activity:

Using the template below, play the Jarabadach game from Africa! (It is like Tic-Tac-Toe!) Before you begin, you can copy the template onto an 8.5" x 11" sheet of paper or cardstock and decorate it. To play, each player has one set of three buttons (or something similar). Take turns putting your buttons on any of the gray dots. When all six buttons are placed on the board, each player takes turns moving their buttons until they get three in a row.

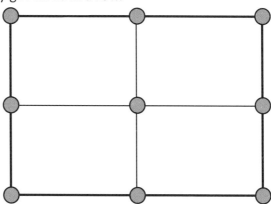

T is for Tribals!

I. The Children's Workbook (page 141, 142):

> **Discuss** the Reflection Question in *The Children's Workbook* for Week 24: Day 2 and have them write down their answer.

Then, look at the Cat and Dog Cartoon and fill in a possible response for the cat and dog. (There is no right or wrong answer.) You'll find the actual cartoon on page 69 in the cartoon book. You may want to use this to guide your child's answer.

> While your child is coloring in the cartoon, **discuss** future dreams and goals and see if they are more Top Line or Bottom Line or evenly balanced.

II. I Heard Good News Today 2: Big Life:

- Find the country of **Nepal** on a globe or the map in *I Heard Good News Today 2: Big Life* on page IX.
- Read Chapter 47, **"Wanting To Die,"** in *I Heard Good News Today 2: Big Life* beginning on page 127.

III. The Children's Workbook:

> **Discuss:** Explain why were the Hindus in Hari's village upset over what God had done?

Pray for missionaries to be sent to the 55,000 Santal Hindu Muslims of Nepal. (Don't forget to review the memory verse!)

IV. Optional Cartoon:

Look up bonus Cartoon #107 in the cartoon book and discuss having integrity.

T is for Tribals!

I. The Children's Workbook (page 143, 144):

> **Discuss** the Reflection Question in *The Children's Workbook* for Week 24: Day 3 and have them write down their answer.

Then, look at the Cat and Dog Cartoon and fill in a possible response for the cat and dog. (There is no right or wrong answer.) You'll find the actual cartoon on page 94 in the cartoon book. You may want to use this to guide your child's answer.

> While your child is coloring in the cartoon, **discuss** where the poor are in your area and something practical that you could do to help them.

II. I Heard Good News Today 2: Big Life:

- Find the country of **Nepal** on a globe or the map in *I Heard Good News Today 2: Big Life* on page IX.
- Read Chapter 48, **"Her Sister-in-Law,"** in *I Heard Good News Today 2: Big Life* beginning on page 129.

III. The Children's Workbook:

> **Discuss:** How did Bhim's sister-in-law make God famous by her attitudes or actions?

Pray for missionaries to be sent to the 2,400 Unreligious Vayu of Nepal. (Don't forget to review the memory verse!)

IV. Optional Cartoon:

Look up Cartoon #62 in the cartoon book and discuss keeping your dresser clean.

Week 25- H is for Hindus

I. Teaching:

Which unreached people did we learn about last week? (T for Tribals!) Do you remember what the H stood for?

> **Challenge:** Today we will learn about Hindus, who mainly live in India. Can you find India on the map?

Hindus believe in many gods (350 million!) and have many rituals as a part of their religion. They burn incense in their homes or in the temples as a part of their worship. Many times a year, festivals to the different gods are held. People have parades and go to the temples or shrines. Even in the temples, people worship individually; it's not like going to a church service.

Hindus do not eat meat of any kind because of their belief in reincarnation. They believe when you die, depending on how you lived in this life, you will come back in the next life as an animal (cat, sheep, cow) or bug or insect. They never kill any bugs or animals for they fear they are killing some relative or friend who has died.

> **Action:** Go find a bug or an insect and try to imagine it is your great-grandma or great-grandpa.

Even though the government has outlawed the caste system, the culture still operates in it. Which caste a person comes from determines what kind of job they can have and with whom they can be friends. Have you ever seen a Hindu woman with a mark on her forehead? The marks can differ in color to indicate which class they come from (lower-middle-upper). They generally don't marry between castes.

> **Discuss:** What do we believe happens to us as Christians when we die? (John 14:2-4)

With Hindus believing in so many gods, the idea of believing in Jesus as God is not difficult to them. Jesus can just be **another** god to them.

> **Discuss**: Do Hindus need to know the one true God?

II. *Memory Verse:*

Our memory verse for this week is Matthew 28:20, "...and teaching them to obey everything I have commanded you. And surely I am with you always, to the very end of the age."

> ***Discuss*** what this verse means with your child.

III. *Theme Song:* (Track 1, *The Children's Workbook*, page 196)

IV. *Prayer to Go:*

Conclude today's teaching with praying Prayer to Go #18, asking to love the one true God with all our heart, soul, mind, and strength.

"Love the Lord your God with all your heart, with all your soul, with all your mind, and with all your strength." Mark 12:30

Dear Lord, help me to grow in my love for You each day. I want to love You with all my heart, soul, mind and strength.

V. *The Children's Workbook* (Page 145, 146)*:*

To finish the day, have your child open to Week 25: Day 1 in The Children's Workbook. Have your student write out the weekly verse and read the story about Madhu, the little Hindu girl.

VI. *Optional Activity:*

Create Indian festival elephants! Before you begin, go online and search for photos of "festival elephants in India." They are intricately and brightly decorated. For the craft, draw a simple elephant shape on white paper (see page 190 of *The Children's Workbook* if you want one to use). Color and decorate your elephant to prepare for a festival, and then cut him out and paste onto some colorful paper. If you have sequins or glitter, use it! You can even create a frame for your elephant poster.

H is For Hindus!

I. *The Children's Workbook* (page 147, 148):

> ***Discuss*** the Reflection Question in *The Children's Workbook* for Week 25: Day 2 and have them write down their answer.

Then, look at the Cat and Dog Cartoon and fill in a possible response for the cat and dog. (There is no right or wrong answer.) You'll find the actual cartoon on page 55 in the cartoon book. You may want to use this to guide your child's answer.

> While your child is coloring in the cartoon, ***discuss*** treating your siblings or cousins kindly.

II. *I Heard Good News Today 2: Big Life:*

- Find the country of ***India*** on a globe or the map in *I Heard Good News Today 2: Big Life* on page IX.
- Read Chapter 49, **"Poisoned Tea,"** in *I Heard Good News Today 2: Big Life* beginning on page 131.

III. *The Children's Workbook:*

> ***Discuss:*** How did Raban make God famous by his attitudes or actions?

Pray for missionaries to be sent to the 4.6 million Rajbangshi Hindus of India. (Don't forget to review the memory verse!)

IV. *Optional Cartoon:*

Look up bonus Cartoon #105 in the cartoon book and discuss how "being blessed to be a blessing" applies to the dog and not the cat. Ask, "Which friend would you want to have?"

H is for Hindus!

I. The Children's Workbook *(page 149, 150)*:

> ***Discuss*** the Reflection Question in *The Children's Workbook* for Week 25: Day 3 and have them write down their answer.

Then, look at the Cat and Dog Cartoon and fill in a possible response for the cat and dog. (There is no right or wrong answer.) You'll find the actual cartoon on page 76 in the cartoon book. You may want to use this to guide your child's answer.

> While your child is coloring in the cartoon, ***discuss*** trying new foods and honoring the hosts.

II. I Heard Good News Today 2: Big Life:

- Find the country of **Cambodia** on a globe or the map in *I Heard Good News Today 2: Big Life* on page IX.
- Read Chapter 50, **"Hold On To Your Faith,"** in *I Heard Good News Today 2: Big Life* beginning on page 135.

III. The Children's Workbook:

> ***Discuss:*** List three things in the Christians' meeting that made God famous in Chheng's eyes:

Pray for missionaries to be sent to the 32,000 Unreligious Campuon of Cambodia. (Don't forget to review the memory verse!)

IV. Optional Cartoon:

Look up Cartoon #66 in the cartoon book and discuss different attitudes we can have while playing sports. Which of those honor God? Which ones don't honor God?

Week 26– U is for Unreligious/Chinese

I. Teaching:

Have you ever eaten Chinese food? Do you know anything about Chinese people?

The **U** in T.H.U.M.B stands for Unreligious people, the majority of whom live in China and are atheists. An atheist is someone who believes there is no God.

> **Activity:** Find China on the map.

China is a communist country whose leaders tell people there is no God. In a communist country, all the people are to do exactly what the government says. The government tries to keep everything equal for the people.

China has the largest population in the world. With so many people to feed, clothe, and house, for a long time the government only allowed couples to have one child.

Even though the government tells people not to believe in God, many forms of Hinduism and Buddhism exist secretly in the country. Christianity is also secretly spreading among the Chinese people with house churches, but very little outreach has been done among the large Muslim population of China.

> **Discuss:**
> - What do you call a person who doesn't believe in God?
> - If the government doesn't allow the people to believe in God, what kind of church would they attend?
> - Would you go to the same house every week to have church if the government was watching everything?
> - Do the Chinese people need to find out about Jesus?

II. Memory Verse:

Our memory verse for this week is Psalm 72:17, "...may his name endure forever; may it continue as long as the sun. All nations will be blessed through him, and they will call him blessed."

> **Discuss** what this verse means with your child.

III. *Theme Song:* (Track 1, *The Children's Workbook*, page 196)

IV. *Prayer to Go:*

Conclude today's teaching with praying Prayer to Go #32, seeking to serve like Jesus served.

> "For even the Son of Man did not come to be served, but to serve."
> Mark 10:45

> *Help me remember that if Jesus came to serve and not be served—that should be my attitude also. Open my eyes to ways I can serve others for Your glory every day.*

V. *The Children's Workbook* *(Page 151, 152):*

To finish the day, have your child open to Week 26: Day 1 in The Children's Workbook. Have your student write out the weekly verse and read the story about Peiling, the little Chinese girl.

VI. *Optional Activity:*

Play Tangrams, an ancient puzzle originating in China and played all over the world. Using the template on page 188 in your children's workbook, copy, decorate, and cut out the seven shapes of the puzzle. You can either make your own pictures and designs with these seven shapes, or you can go online and look up specific puzzle designs to try and make.

Tangram rules:

1. Each puzzle must use all seven shapes.
2. Each shape must touch at least one other shape.
3. Shapes must not overlap.

U is for Unreligious/Chinese!

I. The Children's Workbook *(page 153, 154)*:

> **Internet:** In the Reflection Question in *The Children's Workbook* for Week 26: Day 2, help them go to the internet and find the answers for the Chinese words. Or if you have a Chinese friend, go to them and ask them in person!

Then, look at the Cat and Dog Cartoon and fill in a possible response for the cat and dog. (There is no right or wrong answer.) You'll find the actual cartoon on page 65 in the cartoon book. You may want to use this to guide your child's answer.

> While your child is coloring in the cartoon, *discuss* taking the effort to do a job well.

II. I Heard Good News Today 2: Big Life:

- Find the country of **Cambodia** on a globe or the map in *I Heard Good News Today 2: Big Life* on page IX.
- Read Chapter 51, **"She Never Felt So Alone,"** in *I Heard Good News Today 2: Big Life* beginning on page 137.

III. The Children's Workbook:

> **Discuss:** What did God use in Sam's life to make Himself famous in her eyes?

Pray for missionaries to be sent to the 2,500 Thai Buddhists in Cambodia. (Don't forget to review the memory verse!)

IV. Optional Cartoon:

Look up Cartoon #53 in the cartoon book and discuss how honoring your parents glorifies God. Discuss how disobeying your parents doesn't honor God.

U is for Unreligious/Chinese!

I. The Children's Workbook *(page 155, 156)*:

> ***Discuss*** the Reflection Question in *The Children's Workbook* for Week 26: Day 3 and have them write down their answer.

Then, look at the Cat and Dog Cartoon and fill in a possible response for the cat and dog. (There is no right or wrong answer.) You'll find the actual cartoon on page 90 in the cartoon book. You may want to use this to guide your child's answer.

> While your child is coloring in the cartoon, ***discuss*** being willing to help around the house and accept new responsibility.

II. I Heard Good News Today 2: Big Life:

- Find the country of **Pakistan** on a globe or the map in *I Heard Good News Today 2: Big Life* on page IX.
- Read Chapter 52, **"Renounce Your Faith or I'll Divorce You,"** in *I Heard Good News Today 2: Big Life* beginning on page 139.

III. The Children's Workbook:

> ***Discuss:*** How did God make Himself famous in Hafiz's life?

Pray for missionaries to be sent to the 622,000 Sansui—Beduoin Muslims of Libya. (Don't forget to review the memory verse!)

IV. Optional Cartoon:

Look up Cartoon #84 in *Because He Liked It!* and learn about a high-leaping kangaroo!

Week 27- M is for Muslims

I. Teaching:

Have you ever seen a woman whose head was totally covered? She was probably a Muslim.

Muslims consist of one-fifth of the world's population. There is only one missionary for every 160,000 Muslims in the world. They call God "Allah" and believe that Mohammed was the last and final prophet from God. They believe that first there were the Jews, but they blew it. Then the Christians, but they messed up, too. So now there are Muslims. The word Muslim means "one who submits."

Muslims must follow the "Five Pillars of the Faith."
1. Reciting the belief that there is but one God and Mohammed is his prophet.
2. Praying five times a day in the direction of Mecca, Saudi Arabia. (Each time of prayer is preceded by washing parts of the body to make them "clean" before God.)
3. Giving their tithe (2.5 percent of their income) to the poor.
4. Keeping the 28 day fast of Ramadan. Muslims do not eat from sunrise to sunset during this time of purification and seeking holiness.
5. Once in every Muslim's life they are to make a trip (hajj) to Mecca, the holiest of holy places to a Muslim.

> ***Discuss:*** Do we, as Christians, believe we must be physically clean before we pray? Why not?

Basically, Islam is a religion of works. At the end of your life, God will judge whether your good deeds or your bad deeds were greater and decide if you should go to paradise (heaven) or hell. To a devout Muslim, keeping all the pillars is important so they can **hopefully** go to paradise.

> ***Discuss:*** Do Christians know for sure where they are going when they die? How do we know? (1 John 5:11-13)

Muslims believe Jesus was a prophet just like Moses, Noah and others. They do not believe he was crucified and rose from the dead. The holy book Muslims use is called the Koran, it contains what Mohammed (their prophet) spoke and some of the first 5 books of the Bible and parts of the four Gospels in our New Testament.

Muslims look at the United States as a Christian country, so everything that we do is what Christianity is all about to them. To a Muslim, you cannot separate who they are from their religion. To be a Pakistani is to be a Muslim, there is no difference; therefore, any American they meet is assumed to be a Christian.

> ***Discuss:*** Is everyone in America a Christian? What things could Muslims believe about Christianity by looking at America that aren't true?

II. Memory Verse:

Our memory verse for this week is Revelation 5:9, "And they sang a new song: 'You are worthy to take the scroll and open its seals, because you were slain, and with your blood you purchased men for God from every tribe and language and people and nation."

> ***Discuss*** what this verse means with your child.

III. Theme Song: (Track 1, *The Children's Workbook*, page 196)

IV. Prayer to Go:

Conclude today's teaching with praying Prayer to Go #19, asking to love others with the love of God.

"Whoever loves God must also love his brother." 1 John 4:21

Dear Lord, help me love others with the same love You have given to me.

V. The Children's Workbook *(Page 157, 158):*

To finish the day, have your child open to Week 27: Day 1 in The Children's Workbook. Have your student write out the weekly verse and read the story about Ehab, the boy from Libya.

VI. Optional Activity:

Create a Muslim prayer mat. (It is shaped like a basic rectangle as seen below.) On a piece of construction paper, cut fringe on both ends and then decorate the middle with geometric designs. Look online for design ideas!

M is for Muslims!

I. The Children's Workbook (page 159, 160):

> **Discuss** the Reflection Question in *The Children's Workbook* for Week 27: Day 2 and have them write down their answer.

Then, look at the Cat and Dog Cartoon and fill in a possible response for the cat and dog. (There is no right or wrong answer.) You'll find the actual cartoon on page 58 in the cartoon book. You may want to use this to guide your child's answer.

> While your child is coloring in the cartoon, **discuss** how withholding toys from others is not being a blessing to them.

II. I Heard Good News Today 2: Big Life:

- Find the country of **Cambodia** on a globe or the map in *I Heard Good News Today 2: Big Life* on page IX.
- Read Chapter 53, **"Please, Just Stop,"** in *I Heard Good News Today 2: Big Life* beginning on page 145.

III. The Children's Workbook:

> **Discuss:** What did Boeu have a hard time understanding and how did it make God famous?

Pray for missionaries to be sent to the 20,000 Unreligious Jarai of Cambodia. (Don't forget to review the memory verse!)

IV. Optional Cartoon:

Look up Cartoon #54 in the cartoon book and discuss ways to get your mom's attention.

M is for Muslims!

I. The Children's Workbook (page 161, 162):

> **Discuss** the Reflection Question in *The Children's Workbook* for Week 27: Day 3 and have them write down their answer.

Then, look at the Cat and Dog Cartoon and fill in a possible response for the cat and dog. (There is no right or wrong answer.) You'll find the actual cartoon on page 40 in the cartoon book. You may want to use this to guide your child's answer.

> While your child is coloring in the cartoon, **discuss** showing compassion to others.

II. I Heard Good News Today 2: Big Life:

- Find the country of **Cambodia** on a globe or the map in *I Heard Good News Today 2: Big Life* on page IX.
- Read Chapter 54, **"When Death Leads To Life,"** in *I Heard Good News Today 2: Big Life* beginning on page 149.

III. The Children's Workbook:

> **Discuss:** Why do you think Buddha didn't answer Ruos' prayers?

Pray for missionaries to be sent to the 3,000 Unreligious Kraol of Cambodia. (Don't forget to review the memory verse!)

IV. Optional Cartoon:

Look up Cartoon #44 in the cartoon book and discuss having a flexible attitude when someone plans something nice for you but you don't like it.

Week 28- B is for Buddhists

I. Teaching:

Can you remember all the unreached peoples we talked about in the last four weeks? What is the last letter in the word thumb?

Today we will learn about the final major unreached people: Buddhists. Buddhists believe there are many paths to God. They mainly live in Asia. There are many different forms of Buddhism and many different teachers (lamas). Meditation is an important part of the religion. People are trying to get "enlightened" through meditation by finding the Buddha-nature (god) within them.

One of the Buddhists' holy books is 70 times larger than the Bible! Many times, young men will become monks, either for life or short periods of time. Monks live in poverty, relying on others to supply their needs. If people give to the monks, they are gaining points with God.

Buddhists often believe you can pray to ancestors who have died and they can help you in this life. Buddhists practice their religion individually as well as going to the temple or shrine. There will be a statue of Buddha in their home or in the temple. Buddha is the one who began the religion.

Buddhism was born out of Hinduism so they believe many similar things, including reincarnation. Buddhists believe you can come back again and again, each time attaining more "enlightenment," thus becoming a better person. Buddhists believe that when you die, you enter Nirvana, as in blowing out a flame on a candle. You exist no more.

> **Discuss:** To whom do Buddhists pray? What do they think happens when you die?

II. Memory Verse:

Our memory verse for this week is Revelation 5:10, "You have made them to be a kingdom and priests to serve our God, and they will reign on the earth."

> **Discuss** what this verse means with your child.

III. *Theme Song:* (Track 1, *The Children's Workbook*, page 196)

IV. *Prayer to Go:*

Conclude today's teaching with praying Prayer to Go #30, asking God to not let us become too busy for Him.

> "Be still and know that I am God. I will be exalted among the nations."
> Psalm 46:10

> *Dear Lord, sometimes my parents and I get so busy we don't have time for each other or for You. Slow us down. Don't let us miss the blessings of knowing You and loving each other.*

V. *The Children's Workbook* (Page 163, 164)*:*

To finish the day, have your child open to Week 28: Day 1 in The Children's Workbook. Have your student write out the weekly verse and read the story about Somjit, the little Buddhist girl.

VI. *Optional Activity:*

Play the Japanese Old Man (Ojisan) and Old Woman (Obaasan) Game. The object of this game is for one person to catch the other when both are blindfolded.

> **Blindfold an "Old Man" and "Old Woman," and have any other players sit around them in a large circle. Give Old Man a small bell and turn both players around several times. Old Woman then calls out "Grandpa!" and he answers by ringing the bell (or responding "Grandma!" if there is no bell). She tries to catch him with outstretched arms, and he tries to avoid her. Roles are reversed when he is caught, and when she too has been caught blindfolds are removed and new players are chosen by Old Man and Old Woman bowing down to the new players they choose.**

> **You can also have students use the Japanese words "Ojisan" and "Obaasan" instead of "Grandpa" and Grandma"!**

B is for Buddhists!

I. The Children's Workbook (page 165, 166):

> **Discuss** the Reflection Question in *The Children's Workbook* for Week 28: Day 2 and have them write down their answer.

Then, look at the Cat and Dog Cartoon and fill in a possible response for the cat and dog. (There is no right or wrong answer.) You'll find the actual cartoon on page 91 in the cartoon book. You may want to use this to guide your child's answer.

> While your child is coloring in the cartoon, **discuss** why the cat is being so selfish.

II. I Heard Good News Today 2: Big Life:

- Find the country of **Afghanistan** on a globe or the map in *I Heard Good News Today 2: Big Life* on page IX.
- Read Chapter 55, **"Bullets Hit The Car,"** in *I Heard Good News Today 2: Big Life* beginning on page 151.

III. The Children's Workbook:

> **Discuss:** How did Musa make God famous by his attitudes or actions?

Pray for missionaries to be sent to the 200,000 Quzilbash Muslims of Afghanistan. (Don't forget to review the memory verse!)

IV. Optional Cartoon:

Look up Cartoon #9 in the cartoon book and discuss respecting a child who is taking a nap.

B is for Buddhists!

I. *The Children's Workbook* *(page 167, 168)*:

> ***Discuss*** the Reflection Question in *The Children's Workbook* for Week 28: Day 3 and have them write down their answer.

Then, look at the Cat and Dog Cartoon and fill in a possible response for the cat and dog. (There is no right or wrong answer.) You'll find the actual cartoon on page 3 in the cartoon book. You may want to use this to guide your child's answer.

> While your child is coloring in the cartoon, ***discuss*** how this world is God's creation and how we should take care of it.

II. *I Heard Good News Today 2: Big Life:*

- Find the country of **India** on a globe or the map in *I Heard Good News Today 2: Big Life* on page IX.
- Read Chapter 56, **"Pack Your Belongings and Go,"** in *I Heard Good News Today 2: Big Life* beginning on page 155.

III. *The Children's Workbook:*

> ***Discuss:*** How did Naresh make God famous by his attitudes or actions?

Pray for missionaries to be sent to the 34,000 Ujia Hindus of India. (Don't forget to review the memory verse!)

IV. *Optional Cartoon:*

Look up Cartoon #46 in *Because He Liked It* and discover something very unique about the Death-Adder Snake's tail!

Week 29- Review
Story of the Bible + THUMB

I. Teaching:

In the first half of the year we learned that we (as individuals) are to make God famous. In the second half of the year, we found out that we are to make God famous among all the nations.

> **Discuss:** Who remembers how many stories there are in the Bible? (Yes—only one!) Do you think you could share that story with someone?

Using the first days of weeks 16, 17, and 18, review the Story of the Bible. Review the introduction (Tower of Babel), main theme (Abraham was blessed to be a blessing), and conclusion (all people groups worshiping God). Keep tying in the theme of making God famous!

Go to the Appendix on page 182, then read and complete the activity, "Faces and Fame Among The Nations.

We know that God's ultimate plan is to have people from every tribe, tongue, and nation knowing Him and His love, but many people still do not know God's truth.

> **Ask:**
> - Who remembers the five major religions/groups who still do not know about God's truth?
> - And how do our thumbs help us remember them? **(Tribals, Hindus, Unreligious, Muslims, and Buddhists)**

If possible with your number of students, plan a game where one child at a time is assigned a particular group, and the rest of the children get to ask questions to help identify who the child represents. Repeat until all religions have been assigned and guessed.

II. Memory Verse:

The verse for this week is Isaiah 56:7c, "...For my house will be called a house of prayer for all nations."

> **Discuss** what this verse means with your child.

III. Theme Song: (Track 1, *The Children's Workbook*, page 196)

IV. Prayer to Go:

Conclude today's teaching with praying Prayer to Go #24, asking God for a teachable heart to hear and obey His voice.

> "Today if you hear His voice, do not harden your hearts." Hebrews 3:7,8

> *Dear Father,, I want to be more aware of Your voice. Make sure that I hear what You are saying and follow You very closely. Give me a heart that is willing to be taught.*

V. The Children's Workbook *(Page 169, 170):*

To finish the day, have your child open to Week 29: Day 1 in the Cat & Dog Children's Workbook. Have your student write out the weekly verse and then, based on the pie chart, have them try to figure out how much of the world falls into each of the major blocks of religions that are unreached. After they guess, give them the correct answers. **(Tribals 6%, Hindus 6%, Unreligious 22%, Muslims 21%, Buddhists 6%; all other religions of the world are 5%.)**

VI. Optional Activity:

The Chinese can count to ten using one hand! Teach your children how to do it and have them practice with you and each other.

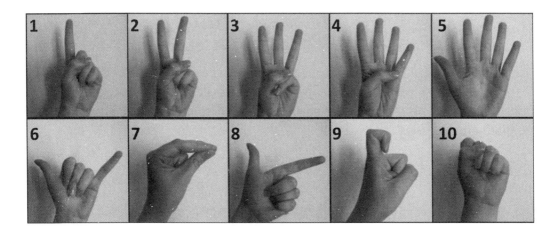

Review

I. The Children's Workbook (page 171, 172):

> **Discuss** the Reflection Question in *The Children's Workbook* for Week 29: Day 2 and have them write down their answer.

Then, look at the Cat and Dog Cartoon and fill in a possible response for the cat and dog. (There is no right or wrong answer.) You'll find the actual cartoon on page 11 in the cartoon book. You may want to use this to guide your child's answer.

> While your child is coloring in the cartoon, **discuss** being patient when playing with others.

II. I Heard Good News Today 2: Big Life:

- Find the country of **India** on a globe or the map in *I Heard Good News Today 2: Big Life* on page IX.
- Read Chapter 57, **"The Day of Salvation,"** in *I Heard Good News Today 2: Big Life* beginning on page 157.

III. The Children's Workbook:

> **Discuss:** List all of the things that were happening that were keeping Preeti from seeing God as famous.

Pray for missionaries to be sent to the 13 million Pasi Hindus of India. (Don't forget to review the memory verse!)

IV. Optional Cartoon:

Look up Cartoon #92 in *Because He Liked It!* and discover what is so cool about a salamander's tongue.

Review

I. The Children's Workbook *(page 173, 174)*:

> ***Discuss*** the Reflection Question in *The Children's Workbook* for Week 29: Day 3 and have them write down their answer.

Then, look at the Cat and Dog Cartoon and talk about the differences between a Cat and Dog in how they respond to the need of the nations. Ask your child if they truly are willing to be used by God to go any where He wants to send them. (This cartoon is not found in the *102 Differences Between Cats and Dogs for Kids*. It was taken from *101 Differences Between Cats and Dogs*.)

> While your child is coloring in the cartoon, ***discuss*** the need for laborers in the Muslim world. In northern India, it is one missionary for every five million Muslims.

II. I Heard Good News Today 2: Big Life:

- Find the country of **Afghanistan** on a globe or the map in *I Heard Good News Today 2: Big Life* on page IX.
- Read Chapter 58, **"The War Movies,"** in *I Heard Good News Today 2: Big Life* beginning on page 159.

III. The Children's Workbook:

> ***Discuss:*** How did Mufti make God famous by his attitudes or actions?

Pray for missionaries to be sent to the 12,500 Jews of Afghanistan. (Don't forget to review the memory verse!)

IV. Optional Cartoon:

Go to Cartoon #65 in *Because He Liked It!* and discover how one of the heaviest animals on earth is a good swimmer!

Week 30- Action Steps

I. Teaching:

We have learned that we are here to make God famous not only to those around us but also to the nations all over the earth.

What are some ways you can do that? How can you be a blessing to the nations?

God wants to use each of you for His glory. Here are some suggested steps of action to join in His work:

1. **LORDSHIP** — Make sure that you know Jesus as Savior and Lord (boss) of your life:
    *   Can you say to Jesus..."I will be anything, go anywhere, and do anything to help send the gospel to the unreached peoples?"

2. **PRAYER** — Pray daily for missionaries or unreached peoples:
    *   Read and pray through *Window on the World: When We Pray God Works*
    *   Pray for and learn about unreached people groups on: http://joshuaproject.net
    *   Choose one missionary family that your church supports and pray for them for the next year. Put their photo on a world map in your kitchen. Add a new family to pray for each year.

3. **THE BIBLE** — Review the memory verses:
    *   Learn new memory verses
    *   When you read your Bible, look for how God was reaching out to "all nations" in the stories that you read, and highlight those verses in your favorite neon color.

4. **AWARENESS** — Look at National Geographic magazines to learn about other cultures:
    *   Read missionary biographies and other books about various cultures
    *   Put a map of the world on the wall in your room and learn about the nations where the unreached people groups live

5. **FRIENDSHIP** — Become a friend with someone from another culture:
    *   Most universities have an international friendship program- call and find out what is available in your area.
    *   Go to a restaurant of another culture and try their foods and eat them in the traditional style, i.e. use chopsticks.
    *   Become a pen pal with a missionary kid whose parents are serving overseas. For information or more ideas, contact Frontiers (1-800-Go2Them.)

6. GIVING — Save 10% of your allowance each week. At the end of the year, send it (or a portion of it) to help support a missionary or special project that takes the gospel to an unreached people group:

- Recycle cans or do odd jobs and give the money to missions

II. Memory Verse:

Instead of a new verse this week, review previous verses and choose four of the action steps to do.

III. Theme Song: (Track 1, *The Children's Workbook*, page 196)

IV. Prayer to Go:

Conclude today's teaching with praying Prayer to Go #25, about making every day count for God's glory.

"Teach me to number my days a right, that we may gain a heart of wisdom." Psalm 90:12

Dear Lord, I want each day to count for Jesus and Your glory. Don't let me waste my time, energy or money on worthless things.

V. The Children's Workbook *(Page 175, 176):*

To finish the day, have your child open to Week 30: Day 1 in The Children's Workbook. Students will complete the "World Christian Inventory" activity page.

VI. Optional Activity:

Tell someone outside of your immediate family (maybe a friend or a grandparent) what you have learned this past year.

Action Steps

I. *The Children's Workbook* (page 177, 178):

> ***Discuss*** the Reflection Question in *The Children's Workbook* for Week 30: Day 2 and have them write down their answer.

Then, look at the Cat and Dog Cartoon and fill in a possible response for the cat and dog. (There is no right or wrong answer.) You'll find the actual cartoon on page 101 in the cartoon book. You may want to use this to guide your child's answer.

> While your child is coloring in the cartoon, ***discuss*** what is really important in life—and what the world tells us is important, that really isn't.

II. *I Heard Good News Today 2: Big Life:*

- Find the country of ***India*** on a globe or the map in *I Heard Good News Today 2: Big Life* on page IX.
- Read Chapter 59, **"The Alcoholic Fighter,"** in *I Heard Good News Today 2: Big Life* beginning on page 163.

III. *The Children's Workbook:*

> ***Discuss:*** What did God use in Raja's life to make Himself famous in Raja's eyes?

Pray for the 220,000 Kuki Christians to be bold and share their faith with the other Muslims and Buddhists in their area. (Don't forget to review the memory verse!)

IV. *Optional Cartoon:*

Look up Cartoon #73 in the cartoon book and discuss different ways of raising money for people who are in need.

Action Steps

I. The Children's Workbook *(page 179, 180):*

> ***Discuss*** the Reflection Question in *The Children's Workbook* for Week 30: Day 3 and have them write down their answer.

Then, look at the Cat and Dog Cartoon and fill in a possible response for the cat and dog. (There is no right or wrong answer.) You'll find the actual cartoon on page 102 in the cartoon book. You may want to use this to guide your child's answer.

> While your child is coloring in the cartoon, ***discuss*** the fact that God wants to reward us in heaven for our good deeds. (Be sure they understand that this has nothing to do with getting into heaven—that is by grace alone.) Deeds done to glorify God will be rewarded. Deeds done to point to ourselves won't.

II. I Heard Good News Today 2: Big Life:

- Find the country of **India** on a globe or the map in *I Heard Good News Today 2: Big Life* on page IX.
- Read Chapter 60, **"He Wasn't Afraid,"** in *I Heard Good News Today 2: Big Life* beginning on page 165.

> **Moms, please note, there are five bonus stories.*
> *Some moms felt these were too intense for grades 1-6,*
> *therefore we use them for teenagers.*
> *But see what **you** think because*
> *others moms said, "No problem!"*

III. The Children's Workbook:

> ***Discuss:*** What did the doctor do to make God famous in Noor Alam's eyes?

Pray for missionaries to be sent to the 1.23 million Teli Hindus of Ghana. (Don't forget to review the memory verse!)

IV. Optional Cartoon:

Look up Cartoon #79 in the cartoon book and discuss having integrity.